HOW YOU CAN WRITE A GREAT FIRST BOOK

A quick and easy guide with sixteen inspirational stories

By Barry Phillips

Published by
Filament Publishing Ltd
16 Croydon Road, Beddington, Croydon,
Surrey, CR0 4PA, United Kingdom.
www.filamentpublishing.com
Telephone: +44 (0)208 688 2598

How you can write a great first
book by Barry Phillips
© 2018 Barry Phillips
ISBN 978-1-912256-84-6
Printed by IngramSpark

Barry Phillips has asserted the right under
the Copyright, Designs and Patents Act 1988
to be identified as the author of this work.

All rights reserved.
No part of this book may be reproduced
in any way without the prior written
permission from the publishers.

"If you have ever thought of writing a book, start by reading this book. Barry Phillips provides writers a masterful and user-friendly guide to understanding the entire process of book writing. All of us have wondered, "Could I write a book?" This book will convince you that you can do it. It will inspire you to do it. And it will elegantly guide you through the entire process of getting it done! "

Dr. Tom Barrett, Worldwide Best-Selling Author

"I have read many books that don't hold up to their title but I can truly say that cannot be said about this one. As a budding author myself, when reading this book I thought the author had jumped into my head and read every thought (excuse) I had about not writing my book. The author is gifted with an amazing talent of making you feel he is talking specifically to you.

Not only has the hard work of looking for information been done for you, but, the 'Why to', and the 'How to', makes it so ABC............ Each chapter is like a little mini book in itself. My gratitude for the information/inspiration and definitely the motivation to start writing."

Bernie Allen, Entrepreneur

"In this engaging book Barry brings to life 20 years of book expertise. He really proves why he is best placed to guide a first time author to success. A must read of anyone wanting to release their inner author."

Francesca Boorman, Entrepreneur

This Book and its Author

"This inspirational book really does show you how to make your first book, great. Barry's unique approach includes sixteen valuable stories, which can have a life changing impact."

Reading this book you will discover how to:

- become inspired to write
- get started on your book
- organise and plan your book
- prepare and research your book
- build your book team
- create a dynamic title with a stand out cover
- develop the mindset of a best-selling author
- publish both an e-book and a 'tree book'
- produce great content that you will be proud to publish, and more…

Barry Phillips is an entrepreneur. His company has sold more than one million self-enrichment and business books during the past twenty two years. Barry coaches business professionals, writers and first time, non-fiction authors who want to write best-selling books.

Table of Contents

Chapter One:	Start With Your 'Why'	**7**
Chapter Two:	Great Readers Become Great Writers	**33**
Chapter Three:	Proper Planning Leads to Proper Results	**51**
Chapter Four:	Do You Judge a Book by its Cover?	**81**
Chapter Five:	The Write Frame of Mind	**99**
Chapter Six:	Are You Writing or Waiting?	**119**
Chapter Seven:	Write Something Worth Reading, or Do Something Worth Writing	**151**
Gratitude		**173**
To You, the Reader		**175**
Further Reading		**177**

HOW YOU CAN WRITE A FIRST GREAT BOOK

Chapter One:
Start With Your 'Why'

In this book, I will share the best and most practical ideas, strategies and stories I have found to help you. I intend to encourage and inspire you to take a risk and write your great first book. You may never know the difference it could make to someone's life. I want to encourage everyone to find their own song and I don't mean necessarily music. By song, I mean our intrinsic individual creativity. Our creativity is so close to us that sometimes we tend to overlook it or even, devalue it.

We somehow adopt the attitude that if it's easy, it isn't worth much; as if, only effort creates something great. Trust your own song! Two decades ago I started to collect inspirational stories from all across the world that inspired both me and other people with their messages. I have shared my favourite stories in this book to either make you stop and think, or to make a point.

Is it Worth the Risk?
Written by Jeff McMullen, a famous American clown.

Back in the 1980s, I had the opportunity to play the character of Ronald McDonald for the MacDonald's Corporation. My marketplace covered most of Arizona and a portion of Southern California. One of our standard events was Ronald Day. One day each month, we visited as many of the community hospitals as possible, bringing a little happiness into a place where no one ever looks forward to going. I was very proud to be able to make a difference for children and adults who were experiencing some 'down time'. The warmth and gratification I received stayed with me for weeks. I loved the project, MacDonald's loved the project, the kids and adults loved it and so did the nursing and hospital staff.

There were two restrictions placed on me during a visit. Firstly, I could not go anywhere in the hospital without a MacDonald's personnel (my handlers), as well as the hospital personnel. That way, if I were to walk into a room and frighten a child, there was someone there to address the issue immediately. And secondly, I could not physically touch anyone within the hospital. They did not want me transferring germs from one patient to another. I understood why they had this 'don't touch' rule, but I didn't like it. I believe touching is the most honest form of communication we will ever know. Printed and spoken words can lie; it is impossible to lie with a warm hug. Breaking either of these rules, I was told, meant I could lose my job.

Toward the end of my fourth year of Ronald Days, as I was heading down a hallway after a long day in grease paint and on my way home, I heard a little voice, "Ronald, Ronald." I stopped. The soft little voice was coming through a half-opened door. I pushed the door open and saw a young boy, about five years old, lying in his Dad's arms, hooked up to more medical equipment than I had ever seen. Mom was on the other side, along with Grandma, Grandpa and a nurse tending to the equipment. I knew by the feeling in the room that the situation was grave. I asked the little boy his name - he told me it was Billy - and I did a few simple magic tricks for him. As I stepped back to say good-bye, I asked Billy if there was anything else I could do for him.

"Ronald, would you hold me?"

Such a simple request, but what ran through my mind was that if I touched him, I could lose my job. So, I told Billy I could not do that right now, but I suggested that he and I colour a picture. On completing a wonderful piece of art we were both very proud of, Billy asked me to hold him again. By this time my heart was screaming, "Yes!"

But my mind was screaming louder, "No, you are going to lose your job."

This second time Billy asked me, I had to ponder why I could not grant the simple request of a little boy who would probably not be going home. I asked myself why I was being logically and emotionally torn apart by someone I had never seen before and would probably never see again.

"Hold me." It was such a simple request and yet...

I searched for any reasonable response that allowed me to leave. I could not come up with a single one. It took me a moment to realize that in this situation, losing my job may not be the disaster I feared. Was losing my job the worst thing in the world?

Did I have enough self-belief that if I did lose my job I would be able to pick up and start again? The answer was a loud, bold, affirming, "Yes!" I could pick up and start again. So, what was the risk? If I lost my job, it probably would not be long before I lost my car, then my home... and to be honest, I really liked those things. But I realized that at the end of my life, the car would have no value and neither would the house. The only things that had steadfast value were experiences. Once I reminded myself - the real reason - that I was there to bring a little happiness to an unhappy environment, I realized that I really faced no risk at all. I sent Mom, Dad, Grandma and Grandpa out of the room and my two MacDonald's escorts out to the van. The nurse tending the medical equipment stayed but Billy asked her to stand and face the corner. Then, I picked up this little wonder of a human being.

He was so frail and so scared. We laughed and cried together for forty five minutes and talked about the things that worried him. Billy was afraid that his little brother might get lost coming home from kindergarten next year without Billy to show him the way. He worried that his dog wouldn't get another bone because Billy had hidden the bones in the house before going back to the hospital and now he couldn't remember where he put them. These are problems to a little boy who knows he is not going home.

On my way out of the room, with tear-streaked makeup running down my neck, I gave Mom and Dad my real name and phone number; another automatic dismissal from MacDonald's, but I figured that I was gone and had nothing to lose. I said to them, if there was anything the MacDonald's Corporation or I could do, to give me a call and consider it done.

Less than 48 hours later, I received a phone call from Billy's Mom. She informed me that Billy had passed away.

She and her husband simply wanted to thank me for making a difference in their little boy's life.

She told me that shortly after I left the room, Billy looked at her and said, "Momma, I don't care anymore if I see Santa this year because... I was held by Ronald McDonald!"

Sometimes we must do what is right for the moment, regardless of the perceived risk. Only experiences have value and the one biggest reason people limit their experiences is because of the risk involved. For the record, MacDonald's did find out about Billy and me, but given the circumstances, permitted me to retain my job. I continued as Ronald for another year before leaving the corporation to share the story of Billy and how important it is to take risks.

Are you letting perceived risks and fear stop you from writing the book you want to get out?

Why This Book?

You may have heard the statement 'everyone has a good book in them'.

A New York Times article by Joseph Epstein from September 2002, reported that 81 percent of adults feel they have a book inside them that needs to be written before they die! I have believed for a long time that most people have a good book inside of them and that most books have an audience waiting for them. The problem for many would be writers, is that they never get started on their book, or if they start they never finish it. Based on this problem I started to ask the question, "Why do people never start or finish the book they would love to write?" This sent me on a journey to find out the answer. My conclusion, after reading over twenty good and bad books on writing a book, attending three weekend seminars and a week-long Writer's Course in Las Vegas, USA, is that nobody has ever made it easy to write a great first book. This became part of my 'why' for writing this book.

The hardest part of writing a book is convincing yourself that it will be worth it, especially when you consider your investment of time and money.

Will You Do It?

Most people collect knowledge and do very little with it. There are thousands of people every year who attend, 'How to Become Successful' seminars, but it's only a very small percentage who actually apply the information to become successful.

"Why is it that of one hundred paying students, attending a 'How to Become a Millionaire' seminar, only a couple will actually take the required steps to achieve that status?"
Jim Rohn, 1930-2009.

The same goes for 'how to' books.

What benefit will you gain from this book if you choose not to apply the information within?

Can You Do It?

Ultimately, there's no other feeling like knowing that your book or books have positively touched and impacted other human beings. My goal with this book is to let you know that whoever you are, you can write a great first book.

- If your spelling and punctuation are poor, you can write a great first book.
- If you only have thirty minutes a day, you can write a great first book.
- If you don't know where to start or finish, you can write a great first book.
- If you only have a vague idea of the message you wish to put out, you can write a great first book.
- If you don't feel worthy of writing, you can write a great first book.
- If you don't really believe you can, you can write a great first book.
- If you're an authority on an industry or subject, you can write a great first book.
- If you have specialised knowledge to teach other people, you can write a great first book.
- If you want to inspire and lead other people, you can write a great first book.

It's my belief that if you follow the easy to understand steps within this book, you will be inspired to take action and write the book you have within you.

I'm not going to say it will be easy. I'm saying it will be worth it. The fact that you are reading this book means you are serious.

Why Me?

I established a company called Knowledge Is King, which in the last two decades has sold more than a million business and self-help books through events, seminars, the website and Amazon. I have helped coach many authors from idea through to finished book, including a couple of Amazon best-selling authors; Wes Linden and Natalie Heeley. In my company role, I have reviewed thousands of books; some great, some good and some I would like to put in the bin and did! I became known as 'Barry the Book' an expert on good books.

There is a reason why the root of the word authority is 'author'.

The Second Hand Bookshop

As a boy I was an avid reader, exactly like my Mum and Dad. We all read every chance we had. Most nights, my Dad was stretched out on the sofa reading, Mum was with her book in her armrest chair and I was off to my bedroom to read. My bedroom was a sanctuary; it was part of an extension that sat above our garage, it felt like a tree house, an escape from the rest of the house and world, a lovely place to read and explore the power of the written word. Books were my refuge. I sat in a trance, lost in the places and stories which books took me to. I have always felt that an author is like a magician; they have the ability to get into our minds and under our skin and they can take us out of ourselves and take us back to ourselves. My genre then was Crime Thrillers. I sometimes read a couple of books a week, which was made possible by a fantastic second hand bookshop we had in town. My routine was to finish school on a Friday afternoon and cycle down to the bookshop with last week's books, ready to exchange them for two different copies. I used to feel so excited by the thought and feel of a brand new book. I still do.

How do books make you feel?

Self-Help

My reading genre changed twenty years ago when I went through a major challenge in my personal life in the shape of a divorce. Although I felt it was the right thing to do, it was not easy. As a couple, we were in the minority by choosing divorce. Most couples stayed together, some to save face, others for the children involved. For nearly a year, I struggled with feelings of guilt and failure that really had me looking for answers. I found all the answers and more in good books and CDs and I began a journey of studying the life-changing works of authors such as Dr Wayne Dyer, Napoleon Hill and Deepak Chopra; and becoming a better person in all the roles of my life. The books helped me to start listening to my inner voice, acknowledging I had done the right thing for everyone concerned.

Which books have influenced your life?

Books Change Lives

This is why I am so passionate about helping people to write their first book. Books have quite literally changed my life, not once but multiple times and I have seen the same result with thousands of friends and customers. Stop for a minute and consider that your book could change someone's life. We have all read books that have changed the way we feel about something or the way we view things. It can be someone else's struggle that inspires us to change a habit or take any other form of positive action. Think about which books have helped to change your life; how grateful do you feel towards the author? Someday, a reader could feel exactly that way about you and your book.

Writing your book will also change your life. It becomes a personal development journey laced with inspiration, creativity and insight. Books help us to understand who we are, they show us how to live and die. A good author makes you pay attention, they make you take notice and this is a great gift. A book is a legacy, which can live forever and generate royalties for the rest of this life and for seventy years after you pass away.

Books can create meaning in people's lives.

My Life Changers

- *How to Be a No-Limit Person*, Dr Wayne Dyer.
- *Think and Grow Rich,* Napoleon Hill.
- *How to Win Friends and Influence People*, Dale Carnegie.
- *The Richest Man in Babylon*, George Classon.
- *Anyone Can Do It*, Duncan Bannatyne.
- *The Top Five Regrets of the Dying*, Bronnie Ware.
- *Jonathan Livingston Seagull*, Richard Bach.
- *The Slight Edge*, Jeff Olson.
- *The Seven Spiritual Laws of Success*, Deepak Chopra.
- *The Alchemist*, Paulo Coelho.
- *The Seven Habits of Highly Effective People*, Stephen R. Covey.
- *Real Love*, Greg Baer.

Which books have helped to change your life?

My Mission

Before I wrote this book, I went looking for a book or a course that would give me the confidence to write my first authored book. I gathered information from most of the books I read and every workshop I attended. I didn't however, have the confidence to actually go on and write this book. Again, I started to study everything else out there, which led me to the conclusion that an easy to read and follow book on writing your first book did not exist. I decided to write the book that you have in your hands. I also made the decision to get the support and help of an author and writing coach, a step I feel is probably a must for ninety percent of first time authors, if you really want to produce something that matters. Although this book focuses on writing a self-enrichment title, the techniques and methods laid out in these pages lend themselves perfectly to other non-fiction categories, including guide books, biographies, memoirs and most types of 'how to' books.

My mission is to inspire other people to go from idea to printed book in their own time frame. I believe a good book is a legacy and that we all owe it to the generations that will come after us to write it.

What's your mission?

Why You, Why Your Book?

Although writing can be hard work, it can also be very rewarding. Writing matters and even though there are no guarantees, you must write. Maybe you want to help other people with your knowledge, advice or experience.

Perhaps you have been successful in something and you wish to tell your story. Perhaps you have been through hard times and learned lessons along the way and you want to pass on the advice you wish someone had given you years ago.

What are your reasons for writing your first book?

Decisions

You will need to make a few decisions before you start.

- Why you are writing?
- Who you are writing for?
- What is your book genre?
- Which category your book will be in, in a bookstore?
- What you want the reader to get from it?
- What you want to get out of it?
- What your book means to you?

You are going to make a lot of sacrifices if you want your book to be good. You will need to plan a serious time commitment to ensure you finish it.

Commit to Showing Up

Motivation comes and goes like a passing cloud. The best way to write and finish your book is to commit to show up every day and continually remind yourself why you are doing it.

You may want to write an inspiring message for yourself and stick it somewhere you will see it when writing. In fact, make several copies of it and stick them anywhere you can see them on a daily basis such as in the kitchen, bathroom, your car, your wallet or purse. Get creative.

Staying connected with your reason why is very important during the whole book writing process.

Ask Yourself the Following Seven 'Why' Questions

1. Why me, why this book and what is my credibility?
2. Why will people read my book and do I know who my audience is?
3. Why is my book good and what is the unique benefit for other people?
4. Why will my book help people and what answers will it give them?
5. Why will people listen to me? Can I tell someone about my book in a single sentence? For example, my sentence for this book is, "This book will take you from idea to finished book."
6. Why will people buy my book and does it have a dynamic title and a stand out cover?
7. Why does my book add value to the world and what problem or challenge does it solve? The value of my first book, Life Changing Quotes, was in having so many great authors and so many great quotes all in one book and in an easy to read format for my readers.

My Experience with the Seven 'Why' Questions

In 2013, when I compiled my first book, I found that after asking myself these seven questions I became very clear as to my 'why' and what I wanted to write. In seeing my answers below you are able to see the clarity I received by answering the same seven questions for my first book, which became an Amazon best-seller in 2016.

1. My credibility was that I had collected life changing quotes for more than fourteen years, from books, magazines, videos and live training seminars.
2. I knew most readers of self-help books would love a great collection of life changing quotes, to be used on a daily basis to inspire themselves and other people.
3. What made my book unique was the fourteen years of research I had done into the difference between a good quote and a life changing quote.
4. My book will give the readers easy access to their own inspiration and also quotes to motivate other people around them into action.

5. My single sentence was, "A book full of quotes that can help to change your life."
6. My cover is of a tiger bunny that is unique and eye-catching and my title, Life Changing Quotes is dynamic.
7. The value of my book is in having so many great authors and so many great quotes all in one book and in an easy to read format.

Write the answers to your seven 'why' questions now before reading any more.

Whose Life Can You Touch Today?
Author unknown. This is an inspirational story that added value to my life and I hope it will inspire you too.

When I was quite young, my father had one of the first telephones in our neighbourhood. I remember well the polished old case fastened to the wall. The shiny receiver hung on the side of the box. I was too little to reach the telephone, but used to listen with fascination when my mother talked to it. I discovered that somewhere inside the wonderful device lived an amazing person. Her name was, "Information, please" and there was nothing she did not know.

"Information, please" could supply anybody's number and the correct time. My first personal experience with this genie-in-the-bottle came one day while my mother was visiting a neighbour. Amusing myself at the tool bench in the basement, I whacked my finger with a hammer. The pain was terrible, but there didn't seem to be any reason in crying because there was no one home to give sympathy. I walked around the house sucking my throbbing finger, finally arriving at the stairway. The telephone! Quickly, I ran for the footstool in the parlour and dragged it to the landing. Climbing up, I unhooked the receiver in the parlour and held it to my ear. "Information, please" I said into the mouthpiece above my head. A click or two and a small clear voice spoke into my ear, "Information."

"I hurt my finger" I wailed into the telephone. The tears

came readily enough now that I had an audience.

"Isn't your mother home?" came the question.

"Nobody's home but me." I blubbered.

"Are you bleeding?" the voice asked.

"No," I replied. "I hit my finger with the hammer and it hurts."

"Can you open your icebox?" she asked.

I said I could. "Then, chip off a little piece of ice and hold it to your finger" said the voice.

After that, I called "Information, please" for everything. I asked her for help with my Geography and she told me where Philadelphia was. She helped me with my Maths. She told me that my pet chipmunk, which I had caught in the park the day before would eat fruit and nuts. Then, there was the time Petey, our pet canary died. I called, "Information, please" and told her the sad story. She listened and then said the usual things grown-ups say to soothe a child, but I was inconsolable. I asked her, "Why is it that birds should sing so beautifully and bring joy to all families, only to end up as a heap of feathers on the bottom of a cage?"

She must have sensed my deep concern, for she said quietly, "Paul, always remember that there are other worlds to sing in." Somehow I felt better.

Another day I was on the telephone. "Information, please."

"Information" said the now familiar voice.

"How do you spell fix?" I asked.

All this took place in a small town in the Pacific Northwest. When I was nine years old, we moved across

the country to Boston. I missed my friend very much. "Information, please" belonged in that old wooden box back home and I somehow never thought of trying the tall, shiny new telephone that sat on the table in the hall.

As I grew into my teens, the memories of those childhood conversations never really left me. Often, in moments of doubt and perplexity I recalled the serene sense of security I had then. I appreciated now how patient, understanding and kind she was to have spent her time helping a little boy. A few years later, on my way west to college, my plane put down in Seattle. I had about half an hour or so between planes. I spent 15 minutes on the telephone with my sister, who lived there now. Then, without thinking what I was doing, I dialled my hometown operator and said, "Information, please." Miraculously, I heard the small, clear voice I knew so well, "Information."

I hadn't planned this but I heard myself saying, "Could you please tell me how to spell fix?"
There was a long pause. Then came the soft-spoken answer, "I guess your finger must have healed by now."
I laughed. "So, it's really still you." I said. "I wonder if you have any idea how much you meant to me during that time?"

"I wonder," she said, "if you know how much your calls meant to me? I never had any children and I used to look forward to your calls."

I told her how often I had thought of her during the years and I asked if I could call her again when I came back to visit my sister.

"Please do." she said. "Ask for Sally."

Three months later I was back in Seattle. A different voice answered, "Information."

I asked for Sally.

"Are you a friend?" she asked.

"Yes, a very old friend." I answered.

"I'm sorry to have to tell you this," she said, "Sally has been working part-time the last few years because she was sick. She died five weeks ago."

Before I could hang up she said, "Wait a minute. Did you say your name was Paul?"

"Yes" I replied.

"Well, Sally left a message for you. She wrote it down in case you called. Let me read it to you."

The note said, "Tell him, I still say there are other worlds to sing in. He'll know what I mean."

I thanked her and hung up. I knew what Sally meant.

Never underestimate the impression you may make on other people with your book.

Whose life have you touched today?

HOW YOU CAN WRITE A FIRST GREAT BOOK

Chapter Two: Great Readers Become Great Writers

It doesn't matter how good your idea is or how interesting the message, if you do not research properly your writing will lack the credibility it deserves. My intention with this chapter is to stress the importance of research and reading. In fact, if you don't read, please don't write. How can you expect people to buy your book and read it, if you don't buy books and read them yourself?

Reading to learn and to improve, introduces you to new information and new knowledge. It opens your eyes to the opportunities all around you. Reading is a common denominator among all successful people. If you have a great story to tell but are not a reader, then consider hiring a ghost-writer. Every successful author I have studied has always researched extensively, or is deemed an expert in the field already, or they become an expert in the process of writing their book. One of the best ways to learn a new concept is to teach it; another great way is to write a book about it. In sharing my own research story and those of several other great authors, I hope that message shines through. And of course, becoming a writer is going to help you become a better reader. I first heard this thought provoking story while listening to Dr Wayne Dyer live at the Apollo Hammersmith in London, where he appeared with Deepak Chopra in their 'Living Without Limits' seminar.

The Cookie Thief
By Valerie Cox as read by Dr Wayne Dyer, 1940-2015.

Dr Dyer was an internationally renowned author and speaker in the field of self-development and spiritual growth. During the four decades of his career, he wrote twenty one New York Times best-selling books.

A woman was waiting at an airport one night, with several long hours before her flight. She hunted for a book in the airport shop and bought a bag of cookies and found a place to drop. She was engrossed in her book but happened to see that the man beside her, as bold as could be, grabbed a cookie or two from the bag between them. She tried to ignore him to avoid a scene as she munched cookies and watched the clock. As the gutsy cookie thief diminished her stock she was getting more irritated as the minutes ticked by, thinking, "If I wasn't so nice I'd blacken his eye." With each cookie she took, he took one too. When only one was left, she wondered what he'd do. With a smile on his face and a nervous laugh, he took the last cookie and broke it in half.

He offered her half as he ate the other half. She snatched it from him and thought, "Oh brother, this guy has some nerve and he's also rude. Why, he didn't even show any gratitude."

She had never known when she had been so galled and sighed with relief when her flight was called. She gathered her belongings and headed to the gate, refusing to look back at the thieving ingrate. She boarded the plane and sank into her seat and sought her book, which was almost complete. As she reached into her bag, she gasped with surprise because there was her bag of cookies in front of her eyes.

"If mine are here," she moaned with despair, "then the other cookies were his and he tried to share."

Too late to apologize she realised with grief that she was the rude one, the ingrate, the thief.

This is a wonderful story, illustrating the power of imagination and the importance of doing your research. It also serves as a reminder of what can happen when we judge other people.

What would you have done in this situation?

My Research

When I started Knowledge Is King, I never realised that my business journey would include twenty years of research into what makes a great book. One of my roles within my company was to review new books. Here is what I always looked for first; I check out the author's biography. I want to know right from the start what their authority is, and whether they are qualified to write on the appropriate level for the subject in question. During the years, we have seen many writers attempt to pass themselves off as more knowledgeable or experienced than they really are. Some of the successful leaders we work with will always ask when presented with a new title, "What has she/he done and have they had any success in our industry?"

It is because some people jump on the bandwagon when they see something going well and write a book to try and cash in. I have come across plenty of these types of authors, as I am sure you have. This doesn't mean that a beginner isn't capable of imparting sound 'how to' advice, but it must be written from the beginner's perspective. This way the reader will identify with the ups and downs of someone starting out.

What gives you the authority to write your great first book?

What Your Readers Want

After more than twenty years in the book industry, I have realised that most people read a book because they want the information it contains. More specifically, they want the benefits it promises because they believe and trust that the author is someone who can give them that. Dr Wayne Dyer shared with me a long time ago these wise words, "Determine who your target audience is; determine what they want and need; and then write a great book for them."

This is exactly what I have done with the book you hold in your hands. I have always believed that everyone has a good book in them, although most people will choose to never do anything about it. Some people will and you are my target audience.

What will the reader get from your book?

The Result of My Research

I started researching what was available to support and help someone write their first book. I read and listened to more than twenty books and audio books on how to write a book and attended three weekend seminars and a week-long Writer's Course in Las Vegas, USA. After all my research, I came to the conclusion that I needed to write this book for first time authors.

Best-selling Authors Research Too

"Become an expert in what you are writing about."
Dr Wayne Dyer, 1940-2015.

Wayne tells the story of how when he wrote, *Divine Love* he had more than 100 books on love in his office, most of which he had studied, during the period he wrote it. A great example of becoming an expert on what he was writing about. Mo Gawdat author of the brilliant book, *Solve for Happy,* bought every title he could find on the subject of happiness. He also attended lectures, watched every documentary and diligently used everything of value he had learned. Where Mo was different was that he approached the subject of happiness from a different perspective than the other authors and psychologists.

This made him unique in a genre that already had a lot of information.

Brian Tracey the famous Canadian author of, *Eat That Frog* said if he was going to write a book on time management, he would read roughly ten books on the subject, listen to six audio sets and attend around six 'Time Management' seminars.

What research can you do for your first great book?

Know Your Competition

Now thinking of your own book, can you answer the following questions? You need to be able to answer them to write a great first book.

- Are there similar books to mine that sell well?
- Are there many books already on my subject?
- If so, what are they? List them for future reference?
- What are the prices of these competing books?
- Is my book unique?
- Do I know who my book will appeal to?
- How big is my market place?

Your research will let you know what else is already out there. You can then separate yourself from everything else. Your research will let you know your competition and your market place.

Do you know your competition?

Google

On the Internet, you need to research your genre in Google and while you are there key in your genre followed by word count. This will give you an idea of the industry standard for the number of words to write. Although I do not believe there is such a thing as a minimum or maximum amount of pages, your book will need only as many pages as it takes to say what you wish to say and you will know when your book is complete.

Amazon

Amazon and Kindle will be your best market research tools. Check out both the United Kingdom and United States of America Amazon websites. Also, check Kindle because some books are only published on Kindle and never make it to physical, printed copy. You can find out the best-sellers in your category on Amazon by searching for a book in your genre and scrolling down the page to view the product details. Below this will be listed Amazon Best-sellers Rank and also a link to the top 100 books in that category. Your research will also give you the chance to see if you have a worthy book and category. Amazon gives you a chance to check out the competition in terms of other authors and what their author rankings are. While researching, check out book titles as well as covers, especially of the best-sellers.

When you check out the competing books always study the Look Inside on Amazon because this can give you a feel for what works as well. You must consider the Look Inside on Amazon for your book because lots of potential customers will view this. You have to grab the reader's attention in the first twenty pages of your book. Part of your Amazon research should also be price. Is it priced for mass-market appeal? If Amazon is discounting a book, this normally means it sells well. Check the Kindle version price at the same time. Is it a lot cheaper? Sometimes this attracts budget or impulse buyers.

Amazon Reviews

Be aware that Amazon gives people the opportunity to be completely unfair and unjust with their reviews; do not take it personally. If they are scathing ignore it; what they think about you or your book is none of your business. Their opinion is simply that - their opinion - and you cannot change it. You write your book to help other people. Focus on the ones who want that help, not the negative ones. You could have ten reviews; eight positive and two negative. Which will you choose to focus on?

Remember the feedback is about your book not about you. Positive reviews will always help to sell books; make sure they are genuine. I have a dozen people who I will send a copy of my book to as soon as it is published, on the understanding that they read it and leave a review on Amazon.

If you want hundreds of positive reviews, start to make it a habit to ask for them and keep on asking for them. For example, "If you feel this book has added value to your book writing journey, can you please give it a 5 star review on Amazon? Thank You."

Increase Your Sales with Your Research

I highly recommend David Gaughran's award winning and best-selling book, *Let's Get Visible*, if you intend to self-publish. There are more than 1.5 million books in the Kindle Store with thousands more added every day. How do you get your book noticed? Visibility is a challenge that requires continual work. But there are tools and strategies to do much of the heavy lifting for you.

In, *Let's Get Visible: How To Get Noticed and Sell More Books*, you'll discover how to:

- leverage Amazon's famous recommendation engine to take advantage of the various opportunities it provides for exposure
- position your books for discoverability on other sales sites
- minimise the time you spend promoting so you have more time to spend writing, and
- promote in a cost effective way that actually works.

By using these tips, you will get your book noticed.

At a Hay House Writer's Workshop in Bristol, they shared current worldwide book sales figures, as below, which you may find interesting:

- non fiction: 70/75 percent book sales and 25/30 percent e-book sales
- fiction: 50/70 percent e-book sales and 30/50percent book sales.

These are rough guides and not exact.

Bookstores

Always research in your local bookstore and the larger ones like Waterstones, if you can. Ask them for books on your subject including the best-sellers. Check out your local library and larger city libraries even if it is only to check titles and book covers. I often spend three or four hours in Reading and Oxford Waterstones shops and have been known to spend a whole day or evening in Barnes and Noble when in the States and Kinokuniya Bookstore when in the Dubai Mall. Sometimes your research can have been your own journey and experiences, especially when you are telling your story. You may be like me in that you have been researching your subject for years, you simply did not realise it.

What is your research action plan for your first great book?

Seven Great Questions to Ask Yourself Regarding Your Research

1. Who is the biggest expert on your topic, in your industry, your country or the world?
   Honestly, ninety percent of new authors do not know the answer to this question!
2. Has your book already been written?
   If it has, how can you make yours unique, better and more relevant?
3. What is the competition to your book?
4. What are the top ten selling books in your main category?
5. What are the top ten selling books in your second category?
6. Who will your book appeal to?
7. Who is going to buy your book?

Now, you are clear on why you are writing, what you are writing and for whom, and you either class yourself as an expert on your subject, are becoming an expert while writing, or you have done extensive research. Be aware of the trap of feeling that you must read everything to be worthy to write your book; research can become addictive. This happens to me if I get stuck; my first thought is I must continue my research.

Mastering a Subject

During the past two decades I have had a fantastic insight into what people will buy when they want to master something. Will you buy only one book on a subject that interests you? How many books do you explore to really understand something? I know from chatting to my customers that they frequently read multiple books on one specific subject if they wish to master it. Here is your market.

Writer's Block and its Avoidance

"The word block suggests that you are constipated or stuck, when the truth
is you are empty."
Anne Lamott, author of the best-selling book, *Bird by Bird*.

Throughout my research authors were continually referring to how writer's block will inevitably happen to most writers at some point. I want to address it from a solution standpoint.

You can avoid writer's block if:

- you have done your research thoroughly
- you make sure you're not distracted when writing
- you are passionate about your subject
- you have a plan that excites you
- you have lots of ideas and material ready
- you give yourself time to read what you have already written, and when
- all else fails, you take a break until you feel inspired again. I go for a walk and although I am not exactly thinking about my book, I quite often return with new observations, ideas and vision.

The story below helps me to always get more from whatever I am reading and I hope it will help you in the same way.

The Four Kinds of Student

In describing the learning process, the Buddhist teachings make use of the metaphor of the cup. Four types of cup symbolise the four kinds of student. Instruction is symbolised by water being poured. The first cup is upside down. This represents a student who is supposedly there to learn, but pays no attention. You may have experienced something similar while reading a book. Your eyes move across the words all the way down the page, but when you get to the bottom, you realise you were daydreaming and have no idea what you read. That's what happens when a cup is turned upside down. No matter how much water is poured, nothing gets in.

The second cup is right side up, but it has a hole in the bottom. We hear what's being taught, but we forget it all too soon. We don't chew on it and digest it, and take it to heart. For example, we might attend a training and when we get home, be asked, "What did they teach?" and we say, "Um, well, it was ... actually I don't remember?" This is the classic case of 'In one ear and out the other.'

The third cup is right side up and doesn't have a hole in it, but the inside is covered with dirt. When the clear water of instruction is poured in, the dirt makes it cloudy. This symbolises the way we can distort what we hear, interpreting and editing it to fit into our preconceived ideas or opinions. Nothing new is actually learned. When we take a lesson, if the instruction matches how we already see things, it is taken as confirmation. Anything new that doesn't match our opinions is resisted, ignored, or is disregarded.

The fourth cup represents the ideal way to be a student. It is upright, receiving what it is taught. It has no holes, retaining what is taught. It is clean, open to learning something new.

Which kind of student are you?

To whatever extent can you be like the fourth cup when doing your research?

Chapter Three: Proper Planning Leads to Proper Results

The intention of this chapter is to help you to understand the importance of planning and to show you how to plan and structure your book. Do not proceed with your book without proper planning. It's like putting on your party outfit without showering first. I came across this next story many years ago. It's a great example of future planning and also, a perfect reminder to not let anyone steal your dream.

Follow Your Heart, No Matter What
Author unknown.

I have a friend named Monty Roberts who owns a horse ranch in San Ysidro, a district of San Diego, USA. He has let me use his house to put on fundraising events to raise money for youth at risk programs.

The last time I was there he introduced me by saying, "I want to tell you why I let Jack use my horse ranch. It all goes back to a story about a young man who was the son of an itinerant horse trainer who would go from stable to stable, race track to race track, farm to farm and ranch to ranch, training horses. As a result, the boy's high school career was continually interrupted. When he was a Senior, he was asked to write a paper about what he wanted to be and do when he grew up.

That night he wrote a seven page paper describing his goal of someday, owning a horse ranch. He wrote about his dream in great detail and he even drew a diagram of a 200 acre ranch, showing the location of all the buildings, the stables and the track. He drew a detailed floor plan for a 4,000 square foot house to sit on his 200 acre dream ranch.

He put a great deal of his heart into the project and the next day he handed it in to his teacher. Two days later he received his paper back. On the front page was a large red F with a note that read, "See me after class."

The boy with the big dream went to see the teacher after class and asked, "Why did I receive an F?"

The teacher said, "This is an unrealistic dream for a young boy like you. You have no money. You come from an itinerant family. You have no resources. Owning a horse ranch requires a lot of money. You have to buy the land. You have to pay for the original breeding stock and later you'll have to pay large stud fees. There's no way you could ever do it." The teacher added, "If you will rewrite this paper with a more realistic goal, I will reconsider your grade."

The boy went home and thought about it long and hard. He asked his father what he should do. His father said, "Look, son, you have to make up your own mind on this. However, I think it is a very important decision for you."

Finally, after sitting with it for a week, the boy turned in the same paper, making no changes at all. He stated, "You can keep the F and I'll keep my dream."

Monty turned to the assembled group and said, "I tell you this story because you are sitting in my 4,000 square foot house in the middle of my 200 acre horse ranch. I have that school paper framed above the fireplace." He added, "The best part of the story is that two summers ago that same schoolteacher brought thirty kids to camp out on my ranch for a week." When the teacher was leaving, he said, "Look, Monty, I can tell you this now. When I was your teacher, I was something of a dream stealer. During those years I stole a lot of kids' dreams. Fortunately you had enough gumption not to give up on yours."

What is your unique dream?

Investing in Your Book

This is the time to bring in an author or writing coach or mentor to help you with the planning of your book. In my opinion this is the best investment you can make in yourself and your book. A good coach will help you to plan your book, will hold you accountable and has previous experience of helping lots of authors to write their first book. Exactly like an architect, a good coach will give you a blueprint to work towards and a structure to actually start writing. However, unlike an architect, an author can and will change their blueprint as the book evolves. When I finally decided to start writing this book after my research was finished, my next step was to find an excellent author coach and approach him or her to work with me. I went through my contacts in the industry and found Wendy who became my author coach. Wendy encouraged me to start with the end in mind, by setting a goal and a timeline to finish this book in three months. Scary, but so powerful and it was a fantastic lesson in how deadlines help people get things and books done! It inspired me and gave me the confidence to get it achieved because I now knew exactly what I needed to do on a daily, weekly and monthly basis and equally important was that I now had Wendy to hold me accountable. Being able to appreciate the contribution a good coach can make and being open to that influence will always make for an easier planning and writing journey and a better completed book.

Going Public

Another great benefit of working with an author coach is it allows you to go public with your writing for the first time in a safe environment. It gives you access to someone who knows the book industry and who is non-judgemental, objective and totally confidential. It is scary, but your writing needs exposure to the eyes of someone who does not know you as a sister, brother, spouse, parent or friend. Someone who will be honest and let you know it's working, or requires more work. The fear of what other people will say can stop many first time authors.

Building Your Team

No matter how capable, talented, efficient or extraordinary you may be, without co-operation from other people, no single person can develop their personal skills. We all need the assistance of a parent, teacher, coach or mentor at some stage. As an example an actor or singer needs musicians, producers and directors and especially an audience, to express themselves successfully, despite their innate capacity for creativity and entertaining other people. Look at most professional golfers, they have a general coach, a short game coach, a mindset coach and probably an agent too!

Another example, is how by flapping their wings in a V formation, geese create increased uplift. This joint effort increases their range by 70 percent more than if they were flying alone. We all need our own team of geese to create a great book.

One of the common attributes of successful authors is their ability to forge strong relationships with other success minded individuals. Their objective is to surround themselves with a team of individuals who can help them achieve their goals. There is nothing that can't be accomplished when the right people work together in any worthy cause. Some of the world's trailblazing entrepreneurs, such as Bill Gates, Steve Jobs, Richard Branson and Mark Zuckerberg had a solid team around them. They knew their team was crucial to their success.

Who will be in your book team?

Structure

As I started to structure my book, deciding how many chapters it would have, I had a picture of it in my mind's eye and as I chose the chapters, most things started to fall into place. My confidence grew because I had a rough blueprint for the whole book. I decided to have seven chapters because the multiple best-selling author Brian Tracey suggests that a good self-help book should have seven, twelve or twenty-one chapters because these are cosmic numbers. I would like to add the number eight to Brian Tracey's suggestion because it is the luckiest number in Chinese culture. If you prepare a detailed plan of each chapter with its sections, more than half your work as a writer is done. You can then fill in the blanks. Although I have a very logical approach to writing a book in that I write each chapter at a time, it's perfectly okay to write your last chapter first. There is no set order; find what works best for you.

How will you structure the chapters in your book?

Stop reading now and consider what your chapter titles will be to give yourself a writing framework.

One Chapter at a Time

I knew vaguely what each chapter would contain, my next step was to start with Chapter One and totally focus on it until it was nearly finished and move onto Chapter Two and so on. All of a sudden instead of the daunting thought of writing a whole book, it seemed like I only had to write seven really small chapters. Spend quality time on your proposed chapters, decide if you really need certain chapters and what should be a chapter or a section of a chapter. Always check you are not saying the same thing twice using different words. Once you know how many chapters you will have, you can start to work out your sub-headings for each chapter and also roughly how many words to write. Most books in the self-help genre have around 35,000 to 40,000 words total with 4,000 to 5,000 words per chapter and 250 to 300 words per page. This can be used as a rough guide, however it's not hard and fast. All good books will have a beginning, middle and an end; and so should each chapter. Each chapter answers a question and makes a point. For me writing one chapter at a time helps me to focus my thoughts and for my writing to flow. I am reminded through sport how powerful doing one thing at a time can be like 'taking one game at a time' and 'one shot at a time'.

What is the key message of each of your chapters?

Chapter Structure

Within each chapter you can work to a narrative arc as below.

- Tell the reader what you are going to tell them. This can be two or three powerful sentences which describe the content.
- Give the reader the information and ask yourself what they will learn and what it will help them to achieve?
- Tell the reader what you have told them in a summary; you can also use bullet points to recap and summarise and if appropriate, include a call to action.

Part of my planning process is to review each chapter when it's finished, or when I think it's finished. This allows me to make sure I do not miss out anything that can help.

Develop Your Regular Writing Habit

Most successful authors dedicate a specific amount of time at the same time each day or week to their writing. What works well for me is to schedule my writing sessions on a weekly basis and to commit to them, in the knowledge that no writing session = no book! As a new author, I know you have to create a writing habit that will work for you and stick to it. Habits are things you do without having to question whether to do them or not. Like you would not question brushing your teeth every day because you have probably done it for many years? Experiment with writing at different times of the day and choose the best time to suit you; only you can work out what is best for you.

I attended a Hay House Writer's Workshop in Bristol and found the author Julia Cameron particularly inspiring. One of the many tips that stuck with me was when she was asked, "How did you come to write forty books Julia?"

She replied, "I set the bar low. As an example, I start writing for only fifteen minutes a day. Make it easy."

What will become your writing habit?

Find Your Inspiration

In writing this book I have experimented with different times and venues. I have written in silence, with inspiring music, in quiet libraries and in noisy libraries. I recently wrote in a Reading Library and found that the second floor was completely empty. Picture this, not only did I have the floor to myself, but I was in the literature section surrounded by all the great literature that has preceded me. It was daunting to be creating something new in the face of all those great authors in that section but it was also inspiring!

Some people write in the morning. Some people write late at night.

What inspires you?

You Make the Time

What I found was that if you develop a daily writing habit it will help you to consistently produce content and that the content will get better. Writing is like exercising a muscle; the more you do it the stronger it gets. I started by writing for an hour on a daily basis, but quickly discovered that I love to immerse myself into a book. I blocked out several hours to write, or I wrote when I was away from everything. I wrote the first few chapters of this book while in the mountains in Turkey on a Yoga retreat for two weeks. We had three hours to ourselves each day in beautiful surroundings and I simply wrote. Nowadays, I write in any spare half hour slot I can find. You have to make the time to write and find what works best for you. When you make the time to write, you can do it anytime, anywhere.

What is your best time of day to write?

The Power of Habit

Yoga is one of my passions and I have a great example of the power of habit from my own practice. In May 2016, I went to a Yoga retreat in Turkey for the first time and as a new Yoga student I was introduced to a 'six minute a day practice' called 'The Five Tibetans' by a fantastic Yoga coach, Kenneth Ryan from Galway, Ireland. Kenny enthused to us that if all we did were 'The Five Tibetans' every day it would change our body and life for the better.

A year and a half later, I am a great testimony to them. Although, in all honesty I never thought I could commit to doing them every day, but I do. The story behind The 'Five Tibetans' is in the book, *The Fountain Of Youth*, by Peter Kelder. You can check out how to do them with Kenny on YouTube by searching 'Yoga Beyond Yoga' if this interests you.

My Game Changer

Taking one step for at least thirty minutes a day, for a minimum of five days a week towards my book, was a real game changer for me, ever since Wendy my author coach got me to commit to it. Many of us have the tendency to postpone even the most important things to the last moment. We assume we will be able to get things done later. But sometimes the unexpected intervenes and everything collapses under the added strain.

When I remain focused I am able to prioritise. I understand that small tasks can be as important as the larger ones and I make sure I get them done at the right time. I make sure I leave time for the unexpected too. This lifts the pressure and allows me to give my best whenever I write. Now even on really busy days I commit at least thirty minutes to my latest book. It can be thinking about it or reading back previous chapters and making changes. Every day I do something. This keeps your subconscious mind working on your book content while you are consciously doing other things in your daily routine. This is, of course, if I have no time, or way of writing, because writing will always be my priority when possible.

Advice from Steven King and Jim Rohn

Best-selling author, Stephen King, when asked, "How do you write?" invariably answers, "One word at a time."

The answer is invariably dismissed, but that's all it is. Writing a book needs careful and thorough planning and the discipline to set and achieve deadlines. Once I had done this, I found that the less I think about writing and the faster I get on with it, the fewer problems I cause myself. Good planning is always helpful, but time spent fretting and procrastinating is a major drain on my energy. I remind myself of this in between writing sessions. Even today I could quite easily have not written because I was not really feeling like it and was unsure where to start. However, I had a deadline to meet for myself and so I chose to write and soon got into a flow. This reminds me of the famous quote by Jim Rohn, "It's easy to do and easy not to do."

Facts Tell, Stories Sell

Work stories into your planning and your book because everyone loves and remembers a good story. Stories are powerful regardless of whether they are true or not. Stories allow the readers to visualise themselves in the information. If you are teaching someone something, nothing is more important than using stories. The reason the world's major religions use stories to teach is because stories are relatable. Make a point and tell a story, or make a story tell a point. I feel so strongly about this that I have crafted at least two stories into each chapter of this book.

Here is an example of the impact a great story can have.

The Seven Wonders of the World

Originally told by Joy Garrison Wasson,
an English teacher in Muncie, Indiana, USA,
more than thirty years ago.

Junior high school students in Chicago were studying the Seven Wonders of the World. At the end of the lesson, the students were asked to list what they considered to be the Seven Wonders of the World. Though there was some disagreement, the following list received the most votes.

1. The Great Pyramids.

2. The Taj Mahal in India.

3. The Grand Canyon in Arizona.

4. The Panama Canal.

5. The Empire State Building.

6. St. Peter's Basilica.

7. The Great Wall of China.

While gathering the votes, the teacher noted that one student, a quiet girl, hadn't turned in her paper yet. She asked the girl if she was having trouble with her list. The quiet girl replied, "Yes, a little. I couldn't quite make up my mind because there were so many."

The teacher said, "Well, tell us what you have and maybe we can help."

The girl hesitated and then read, "I think the Seven Wonders of the World are:

1. To touch...
2. To taste...
3. To see...
4. To hear...

She hesitated a little and added...

5. To feel...
6. To laugh...
7. And to love."

The room was so quiet you could have heard a pin drop.

May this story serve as a gentle reminder to all of us that the things we overlook as simple and ordinary are often the most wonderful and we don't have to travel anywhere special to have these experiences.

What is your special story?

'How To'

As well as a story, also plan to have at least one major 'how to' in each chapter; remember what impacted you on your journey and share this. Always be thinking how will this help the reader? Always express your ideas in an organised and clear way. It needs to have enough real information to be a book rather than a magazine article. Another great tip is when in doubt, put it in.

Dedicating Your Book

Most authors have a special person who has helped and inspired them on their author journey. You may wish to dedicate your book to somebody who has impacted your world. A dedication is normally at the front of the book. It can be short and to the point, simply sharing the name of the special person or people. Or you may wish to write something a little more meaningful. There is no right or wrong way with dedications; it is an individual choice.

Beta Readers

A beta reader (also known as a pre-reader) is a non-professional reader who reads a written work with the intent of looking through the material to give you feedback, as well as any suggestions to add value to your book. I have done this by working with two new authors who are in the process of writing their own first books; Fran Boorman and Bernie Allen. I had sent them my chapters as I wrote them, asking them for feedback and also, if any of the material had helped them with their own books. After sending them my first two chapters Fran told me that my honesty about my divorce had spoken to her personally. Bernie extended her research based on what I had said and discovered that her book title was already being used by somebody on Amazon in the USA. She consequently changed her title.

My intention is to help inspire them both to write their best book and in doing so, I will get good feedback from other authors.

Who can be your beta readers?

Testimonials

Plan to gather Testimonials before you publish your book, providing praise for you and the book and what the reader will get from it. There are lots of different views on Testimonials. Some authors go for quantity, having them on the front cover, back cover and inside the first couple of pages. Other authors value quality above quantity and have a few well-worded Testimonials from high profile people. I favour quality; one well-worded Testimony on the front and back cover preferably from a recognised authority. Any other Testimony that says something genuine and of value I will put on a page at the front of the book. A powerful Testimony will boost sales.

Beware of including too many however. Pages and pages of over enthusiastic words written by people nobody is likely to know can backfire. Be mindful too, if two Testimonials have a similar message, choose the one you feel your readers will resonate best with.

Who will you get to write your Testimonials?

Acknowledgements

If you are going to acknowledge anyone and everyone who has helped you on your journey like your author coach, editor, publisher, your beta readers, any industry colleagues, friends or family, always get their written permission to use their proper name first and put it at the back of the book not the front. The main reason for this is the Look Inside feature on Amazon, which needs to sell your book. Use it wisely.

Who do you need to acknowledge?

Building a Platform

It is also worth considering having a social media plan put together, building a following and getting people excited about your upcoming book. It is important to build momentum before the release of your book if you can. Part of this plan could be asking, "Who do you know who loves your book and has a large social media network?" Some authors start putting excerpts from their books onto social media. If you consider this action, always make sure it's something the reader will benefit from. Be consistent across all platforms, including Twitter, Facebook, LinkedIn and Instagram.

Build your book brand before you launch your book so you have an instant sales market to sell to. The bigger your platform the more likely a well-known publisher will be interested in your book. When Hay House is looking at an author, their first two questions are, "What's your niche?" and, "Do you have a platform within your niche?" They also encourage all their authors to read, *Platform* by Michael Hyatt. I also strongly recommend this book.

How big is your platform?

Planning Your Pricing

There are no hard and fast rules to pricing either your e-book or your 'tree-book'. I think you should price on quality, not on book length, and charge what you would be happy to pay for it. Be realistic and fair. If you are, then why should anyone believe your book is worth more or less than what you, the author thinks?

In my role during the past two decades as the book reviewer for Knowledge Is King, I got a feeling for what the correct retail price should be on most books. Most first time authors however, have no idea and sometimes make the mistake of pricing the book too high, which sometimes discourages the potential reader from purchasing it. Ask your book coach or publisher for their advice and they will help you. As a general rule, the raw cost of printing your book should not be more than 20 percent of the retail price. Also do your research and find out what price other authors in your genre are selling for.

What will be the price of your book?

Author Page

Whenever possible create an Author page, especially on Amazon. It makes things official. You are an author! It gives you a chance to share your biography and to create a great profile and also, to direct customers to your website.

Foreword

Another aspect of your book to consider is getting someone to write a foreword for you. You have to decide. My advice is if you can get a known authority and expert in your field or on your subject, or a celebrity who most people will know, then it's worth it because it builds trust. If you use someone to provide a foreword, make sure they add value and they focus on the main benefits of your book. Never pay anyone for a foreword and reward them by letting them add their website address or an email address.

Do you want a foreword to your book and if so from whom?

There Are as Many Ways to Write as There Are Writers

John Grisham as a young father and lawyer had very little time to write. His desire to write however was so strong that he committed to write for between thirty minutes and an hour every day by getting up in the early hours of the morning. His goal was to write a page a day for 365 days. Three years later his first book, *A Time To Kill* was published. As you may know, it went on to become a best-seller and he went on to become a multiple best-selling author.

Ultimately, the only person who can teach you about writing is yourself.

Create a plan and stick to the plan. There is nothing worse than the penalty taker who decides at the last second to go for the other corner and misses.

I remember the impact the following story had on my author journey and the changes it helped me to make. I hope it helps you too.

What Would You do if You had Only One Month to Live?
Author unknown.

Saturday evening had been fun. We had eaten pizza together, listened to some good music and now we were sitting in the back yard of Laura's house. The summer was hot and many hours after the sunset it was still pleasantly warm.

We looked at Laura.

"What do you mean? One month to live? Why do you ask? Oh please, don't say that you..."

"No, no, no!" Laura laughed, "I'm perfectly healthy and all right. But my neighbour told of a relative who went to a routine check-up with the doctor and suddenly heard he only had one month to live. Imagine! One month left!"

"Oh, how horrible..." We all felt compassion for the man.

"So, I began to think about what I would do if I had only one month to live." Laura said.

We sat there sipping self-made lemonade, Laura's speciality and said nothing.

Laura took out a notepad and a pen and said to us, "Write down what you would do, just out of curiosity."

We tried to protest, but Laura would not give up.

"No, seriously! Imagine how you would feel if you were told you only had one month to live. You would certainly want to do something important with the time you have left! What is it? Don't you want to know what you would really, really, want to do? Three things! We are always

complaining how we would be happy, if only... So, what are those things that would make you happy? The things you would absolutely want to do?"

Reluctantly, we took the notepad and pen and for a while nobody spoke. We all wrote something, tore the page and gave the notepad and pen to the next person. Then we looked at Laura.

"Now what?"

She smiled.

"Now, go out and do those things!"

We looked at her, speechless.

"Yes, don't you see? What did we talk about the whole evening? How we have time for nothing else but work, work, work all the time. Taking care of other people's needs, building other people's businesses. We all come home tired in the evenings and all we have energy for is to eat, do the laundry and flop on the sofa to watch television. What happened to the dreamers we all were at school? You, Mark, weren't you supposed to become an archaeologist? Our very own Indiana Jones?"

"Yea, but..."

"And Tina. You were supposed to put up a shop selling clothes you yourself made. What happened? How did you end up as an accountant? You had such talent!"

"Well, accounting pays the bills..."

"The bills..." Laura almost snorted. "It seems we all live only for the bills. Where are all our dreams? You want to hear what I wrote?"

We mumbled in agreement, a bit taken aback by her excitement.

"My three things to do if I had one month to live," Laura cleared her throat. "One: travel to Rome, Italy and sit on the Spanish Steps toasting to life with champagne. Real champagne, mind you. Two: take all my photos and write stories about them. Who is who, what was good about them and why the photo was taken. Three: sell my house and use the money to have the greatest funeral party ever, while I was still alive."

We nodded in agreement for the first two and laughed at the third. It sure sounded like Laura, that one. She loved throwing parties and inviting people over.

"Now the rest of you."

We read what we had written. The things we would do if we had one month to live. Call all our family members and friends and tell them we loved them. Travel to Hawaii and watch the sun set. Go to see a real volcano. Write a novel. Go to the opera. Paint scenery we loved. Donate money to a charity. Buy a new car. Read the Bible from cover to cover. Meditate in a Buddhist centre. Plant trees. Read that archaeology book that had been collecting dust for years.

When the last one of us had finished reading, Laura looked at us.

"Did you listen to what you just said? All those things are things you could do right now. So, why don't you? Why have you built mental walls around you that stop you from living life as you would really want?"

We sat in the soft, warm night, with the stars twinkling above us, the soft wind caressing our cheeks and hair. No one said a thing. Then Laura got up.

> *"You know. I think I'll go check the travel agencies on the net and book myself a trip to Rome. Want to come along, Jim? I'm sure there are trips to Vesuvius or Etna being sold there too?"*
>
> *Mark got up too, to follow Laura and Jim.*
>
> *"I'll come too. Maybe you can let me check archaeology courses when you've booked your trip."*
>
> *They left and the rest of us looked at each other.*
>
> *"I think I'll go buy some saplings tomorrow,"* Helen *said.*
>
> *"I'm sure I still can find my mother's Bible... I think Janet put it in a box in the attic..."* Henry said.
>
> *For some reason Karen had a leaflet about the local Buddhist centre in her pocket and now she was reading it. And I thought about all the notes I had made to write a novel. Yes, tomorrow I would start.*
>
> *We all have lost loved ones. Family members, friends, neighbours...etc.*

It makes you think, doesn't it? It makes us realise how valuable every single day is. Yet, most of us are so stuck in our everyday routines that we don't even question what we are doing anymore.

Chapter Four: Do You Judge a Book by its Cover?

The intention of this chapter is to impress on you the importance of a dynamic title and a stand out cover with real life examples. A dynamic title and an eye-catching cover are the foundations of your book. It's a well-kept secret in the book industry that great titles often are not the author's inspiration. They come from the team behind the book. Often dozens, sometimes hundreds of titles are viewed and discarded before everyone finally agrees on the perfect title. Spend quality time in your local bookstore looking at the new book section. Take note of your reaction to the titles of books by authors you are not familiar with. You'll see how many books don't tempt you to pick them up due to their titles and which titles intrigue you enough to pick them up and investigate further. This can become a great exercise if you are looking to kill some time in an airport.

I have a fantastic story that will explain the difference a dynamic title can make.

A Juicy Story

Jason Vale, the 'Juice Master', is the best-selling author of twelve books and soon to be thirteen about health, addiction and juicing. His books have collectively sold more than three million copies, been translated into many languages and continue to inspire people from all around the world to take their health into their own hands.

Originally Jason was writing The Big Book of Juicing, which contained the science behind which particular fruit and vegetables would be best for which conditions and all the scientific studies that had been conducted on juicing and fruits and vegetables for health. Jason's publishers at the time, Harper Collins asked Jason for a juice programme that people could do as part of the book. The publishers knew that to make this a successful book, they needed a promise on the cover and this would be related to the juice programme.

At the time, Jason had been trialling a 7 day juice plan that he and several others had completed. The publishers asked what the results were and in particular how much weight was the average weight loss. Jason told the publishers the average weight loss was 7lbs and the publishers looked very happy indeed! They had heard what, to them, was a dynamic title; 7lbs in 7 days.

The next day, Jason received an email from Harper Collins requesting to put The Big Book of Juicing to one side and instead bring out a smaller book called, 7lbs in 7 days, Juice Master Diet. Initially, Jason was incredibly resistant to this idea because he fundamentally does not believe in going on a diet, but in changing your diet. However, after much debate with the publishers, they convinced Jason to launch the new book, after they agreed to include an important amount of psychology within the book as well as a Phase 2 and a Phase 3. This ensured there was a solid follow on plan after the 7 days and there was sufficient substance within the book for people to make a positive lifestyle change following the 7 day plan. The book, 7lbs in 7 days, was launched in 2006 and it is the only juice book to hit the Amazon Number 1 best-seller of all Amazon books. It has remained Number 1 in its category for more than a decade and has been translated into many languages and is an international best-seller. It knocked, The Da Vinci Code off the Amazon Number 1 spot and the book and its App continue to dominate the charts in the food and drink category.

Hundreds of thousands of people from all around the world have now done the programme and have gone on to transform their health and lose a tremendous amount of weight after the momentum that can be achieved in just 7 days.

Create a Dynamic Title

For me this is a non-negotiable. I really feel you must have a dynamic title because it's the first thing a reader notices about your book. Your title should stop people in their tracks and make them pick your book up for a closer look. It needs to tell them what it's all about and create a desire to take action. A great self-help title, for example must include a benefit. This is anything that can make the reader's life better. Remember, whenever someone picks up a book they unconsciously ask, "What's in it for me?" So, you must answer this question with either your title or your sub-title.

Amazon will use the keywords within your title to provide relevant results to their customers. It is vital that you consider the types of keywords your target audience is likely to search for and include them in your title or sub-title if possible. In 2014, I attended a fantastic Writer's Workshop in Las Vegas for four days and for me the highlight and the most valuable lesson learnt was from the English author, Nicholas Boothman who wrote, *How To Make People Like You In 90 Seconds or Less*. He held a whole workshop on the importance of creating what I call a dynamic title. These will sell books regardless of the content and have been proven over time historically. I am going to give you the seven elements of a dynamic title and explain them in more detail with examples that have become best-sellers internationally.

The Seven Elements of a Dynamic Title

1. It tells you what the book is all about, for example, *How I Raised Myself From Failure To Success In Selling* by Frank Bettger and, *The Seven Habits Of Highly Effective People* by Steven Covey.

2. It promises a big reward and tells the reader what's in it for them, for example, *How To Win Friends and Influence People* by Dale Carnegie or, *Your Best Year Yet* by Jinny Ditzler.

3. It says something provocative that offers hope, for example, *How To Make People Like You In 90 Seconds or Less* by Nicholas Boothman or, *Change Your Life In Seven Days* by Paul McKenna.

4. It creates curiosity, which makes people pick it up, for example, *What To Say When You Talk To Yourself* by Shad Helmstetter or, *The Top Five Regrets of The Dying* by Bronnie Ware.

5. It is catchy and easy to remember, for example, *Think And Grow Rich* by Napoleon Hill (nobody

who sees the title, *Think And Grow Rich* can resist looking through its pages and being curious as to whether we can achieve our dreams simply by thinking rich) or, *Attitude Is Everything* by Jeff Keller.

6. It works well as a headline and tells the reader what they will get, for example, *Feel The Fear And Do It Anyway* by Susan Jeffers or, *Being Happy* by Andrew Matthews.

7. It can be read from ten feet away and it attracts attention easily, for example, *The Secret* by Rhonda Byrne or, *Women Who Love Too Much* by Robin Norwood.

Each title stands out and stands out so much that it has practically entered the language as a phrase, in fact some have.

What is your dynamic book title?

Brainstorm Your Title

Cheryl Richardson is the author of the New York Times best-selling books, *Take Time for Your Life*, *Life Makeovers* and, *Stand Up for Your Life*. Her work has been featured widely in the media, including on the Today Show, Good Morning America, The New York Times and O Magazine. Cheryl led the Lifestyle Makeover Series on the Oprah Winfrey Show. Cheryl was the keynote speaker at one of the Hay House Writer's Workshops I attended in London, where she shared her own dynamic title story. Her New York Times best-selling book, *Take Time For Your Life* was originally going to be called, *Make Time For Your Life*. They changed one simple letter, yes one letter and in Cheryl's opinion this made the whole difference.

Get your title right and give it plenty of thought. I love to brainstorm with my books and with the authors I work with. It can be great fun. However, make sure you do it only with people you can trust.

Twenty-one Powerful Words to Put in any Book Title

1. How To...
2. The Power of...
3. Become...
4. Change...
5. The Master...
6. Unlock...
7. The Seven...
8. The Key to...
9. Think...
10. Overcome...
11. Start...
12. Learn to...
13. Unleash...
14. Secrets of...
15. What...
16. The Laws or Law...
17. The Top...
18. The Easy Way...
19. You...
20. The Secret to...
21. Take...

Which of these words will you use in your title?

Your Subtitle and What the Reader Will Get

Your dynamic title grabs the reader's attention and tells them what your book is about. Your sub-title must tell the reader what they will get when they read your book, the key benefits, or your unique approach.

Here are five great examples of the promise of a great sub-title:

- *Rich Dad Poor Dad: What the Rich Teach Their Kids About Money That the Poor and Middle Class Do Not,* Robert Kiyosaki.
- *Just Get on with it: A Caring Compassionate Kick Up The Ass!,* Ali Campbell.
- *Mindset: Changing The Way You Think To Fulfil Your Potential,* Carol Dweck.
- *Don't Sweat the Small Stuff and It's All Small Stuff: Simple Ways to Keep the Little Things from Taking Over your Life,* Robert Carlson.
- *Who Moved My Cheese? An Amazing Way to Deal with Change in Your Work and in Your Life,* Dr Spencer Johnson.

Create an Eye Catching Cover

Remember, you never get a second chance to make a first impression. People often do judge a book by its cover. They will judge your front cover, your back cover and the interior layout of your book. The cover is your 'wow!' factor, it must stand out. If your cover isn't eye catching and engaging, especially as a thumbnail, the potential reader or casual shopper in a bookshop may pass it by without a second glance.

A cover can look brilliant in its full size, but in e-book format it will lose its detail if it is too busy with words and colours. Less is quite often better. Again do your research; check what stands out on the web and what stands out in the bookshelves of your bookstore and library. Also, check what would stand out on a table full of books, which they do in Waterstones shops. Take your telephone with you and take pictures of what stands out for you. Also, take a tape measure to get a feel for what size you would like your book to be. Another way to find out what works is to look at the covers of the best-sellers. What do they have in common, colour, size and font?

Selling Your Book on the Back Cover

Your back cover content is vitally important too. This is your shop window, a chance to market yourself and your book. I have sat for a couple of hours in my local bookshop and observed people examining books. Most people will look briefly at the front cover before turning it over to read in a lot more detail, the back cover. If they are still interested they will start to look inside. Use bullet points to tell the reader what they will achieve as a result of reading your book. This should encourage them to buy your book. Look at my back cover as an example.

The majority of your potential readers will not have heard of you until they find your book online or in a bookshop. Therefore, your back cover should also tell the reader a little bit about you and your authority in writing the book. If you wish to have a thumbnail photo of yourself, put it on the outside back cover. Some publishers recommend no more than 160 words on your back cover biography.

Go Professional

Never try and save money on your cover design; have it professionally designed and professionally proofread and edited. It is worth working with a good graphic designer who specialises in book covers. Please do not try and create your own cover. Remember e-books only require a front cover. Ask yourself does my cover look professional? This is an area that a lot of people can make mistakes with, which can cost book sales in both the short-term and the long-term.

Do You Need a Selfie?

I have a good friend who is working on her first book and when she showed me the mock-up of the cover she had a lovely front and back cover designed both with quite large pictures of herself. I asked if she could maybe take one of the pictures out and put the space to better use and she did. I like the idea of a picture, if you intend to use your book as a business card and you are classed as an expert on your subject with an intention to speak and train or coach on the topic. Ask yourself the question, "Is my picture relevant or is it my ego that wants it there?"

Get a professional head and shoulders colour photo taken for your book cover. It is worth the investment and think of all the time you have put into your book. Never scrimp and save on this critical element. 'People buy books from people.' Readers want to see who you are and feel they know you!

Whose Material is it Anyway?

We should all celebrate other authors' successes and recommend good books by other authors whenever possible. It will be of value to your reader. If you do use anyone else's material in your book always get written permission; this is both a legal requirement and a mark of respect. Apart from which, when you quote other people you add to your own credibility and authority as an author. When you publish your book your rights as the author are protected by the Copyright, Designs and Patents Act, 1988.

Whose credibility can add value to your book?

I share this next story with you as a reminder of how easy it can be to judge a book by its cover.

The Tattooed Homeless Man

By Susan Fahncke, Utah, USA, author of *Angel's Legacy*, the story of her sister's incredible journey through life.

He was scary. He sat on the grass with... his cardboard sign, his dog... actually his dog was adorable... and tattoos running up and down both arms and on his neck. His sign proclaimed him to be 'stuck and hungry' and to please help. I'm a sucker for anyone needing help. My husband loves and hates this quality in me. It often makes him nervous and I knew if he saw me right now, he'd be nervous. But he isn't with me right now.

I pulled the van to a stop and in my rear view mirror I contemplated this man, tattoos and all. He was youngish, maybe forty. He wore one of those bandannas tied across his head, biker or pirate style. Anyone could see he was dirty and had a scraggly beard. But if you looked closer, you could see that he had neatly tucked in the black T-shirt and his things were in a small, tidy bundle. Nobody was stopping for him. I saw the other drivers take one look and immediately focus on something else... anything else.

It was so hot out. I saw in the man's very blue eyes, how dejected and tired and worn out he felt. The sweat was trickling down his face.

As I sat with the air-conditioning blowing, I remembered the quote, "Never judge a book by its cover."

I reached down into my purse and extracted a ten dollar bill. My twelve year old son, Nick knew right away what I was doing. "Can I take it to him, Mom?"

"Be careful, honey." I warned and handed him the money. I watched in the mirror as he rushed across to the man and with a shy smile, handed it to him. I saw the man, startled, stand up and take the money, putting it into his back pocket. "Good," I thought to myself, "now he will at least have a hot meal tonight." I felt satisfied, proud of myself. I had made a sacrifice and now I could go on with my errands. When Nick got back into the car, he looked at me with sad, pleading eyes. "Mom, his dog looks so hot and the man is really nice." I knew I had to do more.

"Go back and tell him to stay there, that we will be back in fifteen minutes," I told Nick. He bounded out of the car and ran to tell the tattooed stranger. I could see the man was surprised, but nodded his agreement. From my car, my heart did a little flip-flop of excitement.

We drove to the nearest store and bought our gifts carefully. "It can't be too heavy," I explained to the children. "He has to be able to carry it around with him." We finally settled on our purchases. A bag of Ol' Roy (I hoped it was good, it looked good enough for me to eat! How do they make dog food look that way?), a flavoured chew toy shaped like a bone, a water dish, bacon flavoured snacks (for the dog), two bottles of water (one for the dog, one for Mr Tattoos) and some human snacks for the man.

We rushed back to the spot where we had left him and there he was, waiting. And nobody else was stopping for him. With hands shaking, I grabbed our bags and climbed out of the car, all four of my children following me, each carrying gifts. As we walked up to him, I had a fleeting moment of fear, hoping he wasn't a serial killer.

I looked into his eyes and saw something that startled me and made me ashamed of my judgment. I saw tears. He was fighting like a little boy to hold back his tears. How long had it been since someone showed this man kindness? I told him I hoped it wasn't too heavy for him to carry and showed him what we had brought. He stood there, like a child at Christmas, and I felt like my small contributions were so inadequate. When I took out the water dish, he snatched it out of my hands as if it were solid gold and told me he had no way to give his dog water. He gingerly set it down, filled it with the bottled water we brought and stood up to look directly into my eyes. His were so blue, so intense and my own filled with tears as he said "Ma'am, I don't know what to say." He put both hands on his bandanna clad head and started to cry. This man, this 'scary' man, was so gentle, so sweet and so humble.

I smiled through my tears and said, "Don't say anything." Then, I noticed the tattoo on his neck. It said, "Mama tried."

As we all piled back into the van and drove away, he was on his knees, arms around his dog, kissing his nose and smiling. I waved cheerfully and then fully broke down in tears. I have so much. My worries seem so trivial and petty now. I have a home, a loving husband and four beautiful children. I have a bed. I wondered where he would sleep tonight. My step-daughter, Brandie turned to me and said in the sweetest little girl voice, "I feel so good."

Although, it seemed as if we had helped him, the man with the tattoos gave us a gift that I will never forget. He taught that no matter what the outside looks like, inside each of us is a human being deserving of kindness, of compassion, of acceptance. He opened my heart. He reminded us all how we do judge a book by its cover.

Putting It All Together

A dynamic title and great sub-title, combined with a stand out cover will compel readers to buy your book. We have all done it; think how many times you have bought a book purely on the promise of how it can solve a personal challenge, manage your money, manage your time better, or become a better parent, partner, or business owner?

Have you created your dynamic title and the ideas for your stand out cover?

Stop reading and do it now.

Chapter Five:
The Write Frame of Mind

Baron Baptiste author of, *Perfectly Imperfect: The Art and Soul Of Yoga Practice*, said he was once the private Yoga teacher to a billionaire. Baptiste asked him how he had become so successful and the billionaire replied, "It was the 80/20 rule; 80 percent was having the right mindset, and 20 percent was having the right skills."

I am a firm believer in both the 80/20 percent rule and the difference having the right mindset can make with writing a great first book.

I love the next story and the message it contains.

The Power of Belief
Author unknown.

There was a business executive who was deep in debt and could see no way out. Creditors were closing in on him. Suppliers were demanding payment. He sat on the park bench, head in hands, wondering if anything could save his company from bankruptcy. Suddenly an old man appeared before him. "I can see that something is troubling you," he said. After listening to the executive's woes, the old man said, "I believe I can help you."

He asked the man his name, wrote out a cheque and pushed it into his hand saying, "Take this money. Meet me here exactly one year from today and you can pay me back at that time."

Then he turned and disappeared as quickly as he had come. The business executive saw in his hand a cheque for $500,000, signed by John D. Rockefeller; then one of the richest men in the world!

"I can erase my money worries in an instant!" he realized. But instead, the executive decided to put the uncashed cheque in his safe. Simply knowing it was there might give him the strength to work out a way to save his business, he thought. With renewed optimism, he negotiated better deals and extended terms of payment.

He closed several big sales. Within a few months, he was out of debt and making money once again.

Exactly one year later, he returned to the park with the uncashed cheque. At the agreed time, the old man appeared. But as the executive was about to hand back the cheque and share his success story, a nurse came running up and grabbed the old man.

"I'm so glad I caught him!" she cried. "I hope he hasn't been bothering you. He's always escaping from the rest home and telling people he's John D. Rockefeller."

And she led the old man away by the arm.

The astonished executive stood there, stunned. All year long he'd been wheeling and dealing, buying and selling, convinced he had half a million dollars behind him. Suddenly, he realized that it wasn't the money, real or imagined, that had turned his life around. It was his new-found mindset that gave him the power to achieve anything he went after.

Remember the truth within this story; you will see it when you believe it.

Sometimes the Only Person Who Has to Believe in Your Dreams is You!

With the right mindset I believe you can write a great first book. Believe in your dreams; constantly redirect your thoughts to why you are writing your book. It is the best way to win the mental battle of writing.

It often takes great courage to speak your truth in a world which provides constant feedback, wants you to be like everybody else and makes you doubt yourself. There will always be someone who doubts you. Never let that person be you. This chapter is all about adopting the right mindset for yourself by looking at the mindset of some highly successful people.

Where Focus Goes Energy Flows

Gary Player won more international golf tournaments in his day than anyone else. When he was competing in a tournament, people constantly came up to him and made the same remark, "I'd give anything if I could hit a golf ball like you." On one particularly tough day, Player was tired and frustrated when, once again, he heard the comment, "I would give anything if I could hit a golf ball like you." Player's usual politeness failed him as he replied to the spectator, "No, you wouldn't. You'd give anything to hit a golf ball like me if it was easy. Do you know what you've got to do to hit a golf ball like me? You've got to get up at five o'clock in the morning, go out on the course, and hit 1000 golf balls. Your hand starts bleeding and you walk up to the clubhouse, wash the blood off your hand, slap a bandage on it, and go out and hit another 1000 golf balls. That's what it takes to hit a golf ball like me."

Here's a similar very short story. A famous violinist was approached by a woman who gushed, "I'd give my life to play like you do." The violinist responded simply, "Madam, I did."

A Powerful Buddhist Mindset Story

I have read this powerful Buddhist story many times. Every time I read this, it comes with a whole new meaning and leaves me with a sense of freedom as I am reminded of the power of flexibility, understanding and more importantly... letting go.

Two travelling monks reached a river where they met a young woman. Wary of the current, she asked if they could carry her across the river. The younger monk hesitated, but the other older monk quickly picked her up onto his shoulders, transported her across the water and put her down on the other bank. She thanked him and departed. As the monks continued on their way, the young monk was brooding and preoccupied. Unable to hold his silence, he spoke out.

"Brother, our spiritual training teaches us to avoid any contact with women, but you picked that one up on your shoulders and carried her across the river!"

"Brother," the older monk replied, "I set her down on the other side, while you are still carrying her."

How would you react in this situation?

Like the older monk... are you able to see beyond your beliefs to help someone in need regardless of what other people may think or say? Or are you more like the younger monk... inflexible and possibly a little judgemental? Holding onto grudges and unable to forgive and move on?

Is there anywhere in your life you can become more flexible and let go of beliefs that no longer serve you?

Is there someone you can forgive who you have been punishing for far too long, especially if that person is you?

Cultivate an Unconquerable Mindset

Mindset is the intangible quality that has more impact on success than talent, education, or IQ. You can't see mindset but you can feel its presence and see its results in the lives of successful people. Look at the presence of Usain Bolt, as an example. Success starts with having the right mindset. It doesn't matter if you are starting a new fitness regime, starting a new business, or coaching a team to a world championship; the psychological principles always remain the same. Average performers quit long before ever achieving their goals. They allow fear and self-doubt to stop them from reaching their highest potential. The common denominators among failures are a lack of mental toughness, a lack of commitment, poor focus and a stagnant mindset.

You must invest the time and effort to cultivate an unconquerable mindset, and while an unconquerable mindset appears innate in top performers, it is actually a set of skills and tools everyone can learn.

What is your mindset?

Consider the following seven elements of highly successful people to help you develop a successful mindset.

1. What you speak you get to keep

Do you ever think the only conversations that matter are the ones you have with someone else? Not quite. The conversations you have with yourself are the most important ones you will ever have. To be clear, we talk to ourselves all day, every day. Eventually, all that robust data adds up to create our individual self-beliefs. Be careful what you say to yourself; plant seeds of positivity and inspiration, rather than criticism and doubt. Your success or failure in anything, big or small, will depend on your programming, what you accept from other people and what you say when you talk to yourself. This is no longer a success theory. It is a simple, but powerful fact. Neither luck nor desire has the slightest thing to do with it. It makes no difference whether we believe it or not. The brain simply believes what you tell it most and what you tell it about you, it will create. It has no choice.

Start by becoming conscious of your inner voice and what it is telling you. In particular, the specific words and statements that it - that is you - use! The more you talk about your book and the business of your book, the more powerful your author's voice will become. While writing sometimes my own inner voice can be negative and my ability to finish depleted. My solution is to inwardly yell, "Stop!" and remind myself, "Every day in every way I am getting better and better as a writer!"

If you feel you need help with your inner voice check out, *What to Say When You Talk to Yourself* by Shad Helmstetter.

2. What are you affirming?

> *"Do not listen to your inner critic,*
> *it has never been published."*
> **Julia Cameron**

An affirmation is anything you either say or think. All your self-talk is a stream of affirmations. You are constantly affirming things to yourself with or without your awareness. Because we have believed something negative about ourselves does not mean there is any truth in it. It can be a lovely experience as you lift the burden of old negative beliefs that no longer serve you and replace them with new empowering beliefs. Affirmations are like seeds planted in soil. Imagine your negative thoughts as weeds and your positive thoughts as beautiful flowers. Now what do you want growing in the garden of your mind?

The more you choose thoughts which make you feel good, the quicker your affirmations will work. So, think happy, positive thoughts; it is that simple.

3. You are a writer

"It is the act of beginning that starts the flow of ideas."
Julia Cameron

You are a writer the minute you put pen to paper or type your first words of your first book. Embrace this, simply be who you are in the knowledge that you are enough and your message counts. One of the things that happens when you start writing is that you will start thinking like a writer. Give yourself a little freedom to develop into something, or someone, you'd actually like to be. Let the book you are meant to write find you. Remember nobody else has your story. As you develop you will start to see everything as writing material.

There is nobody who can determine what you can achieve except you!

4. Believe it and you will become it

Think and behave like someone who is serious about what they do. To be a writer you have to write. When I started my writing process, I started to first think of myself as a writer but I very quickly realised that it was more powerful to see myself as the author I wanted to be, as a published author. You need to shift your thinking from being a writer to being a published author. A way to do this is through affirmations and positive self-talk. So, when asked, "What do you do?" I now reply, "I am an author." This felt really strange at first, however after saying it to other people now more than thirty times, I started to not only feel comfortable with it, but I also, believe it.

In the beginning, I also wrote several pages of affirmations to myself in my journal; like writing lines in detention at school, to shift my mindset from being a writer to becoming an author.

- I am an author.
- I am an author.
- I am an author.
- I am an author.
- I am an author.
- I am an author.
- I am an author.

There can be many reasons why people don't claim the title of author. One reason is if they do stake a claim to the title, it requires them to actually write. The flip side of this is that when you claim the title of author, the magic starts to happen.

Try it; it works!

5. Visualise your intentions

Your intentions set the tone for how skilfully you navigate personal and professional success. Have you set yours high enough to challenge the status quo? If not, think bigger and push past your comfort zone. Get comfortable being uncomfortable. Setting your sights high and believing in the most remarkable outcomes, you can attain changes to the way you show up in the world. Believe me, no one has ever regretted embracing the power to think big.

- Visualise the finished book, your end result.
- Visualise yourself as a published author.
- Visualise handing a signed copy of your book to an eager reader.
- Visualise the difference your book might make to other people's lives.

Enjoy and remember these feelings.

Here's my intention. I'm driven to become a better writer every day, to put out books, which will entertain, educate and inspire.

6.   Grit

Writing isn't a sprint; it's a marathon. The ability to hang on when everything seems to be falling apart around you is a major difference between winners and losers.

> *"Talent counts, but effort counts twice."*
> **Angela Duckworth, author of Grit and world-renowned psychologist.**

Have you got grit?

If not, know this. Both passion and perseverance are vital to your long-term success. Experiencing initial excitement when deciding to pursue a New Year's resolution is quite common. Less common and far more difficult is the sustained focus and drive - throughout long periods of time - needed to achieve it. Grit helps us push past the desire to give up, especially when things get rough. Tough times are par for the course for those people who achieve big things. Without difficult times and failures, there is no learning, no growth. Nothing worth achieving comes without some struggle. Understand the difference between suffering and struggling. Fortunately, grit can be learned and continually developed over time.

7. Execution

Creating a strategy is one thing, but executing it is another. There will always be a million reasons not to write. Decide in advance that taking strong action will be the litmus test for your success. Sure, there will be days when you won't feel like writing or perhaps even be discouraged; too bad.

A professional shows up and does the work, even when they're sick, tired, or busy with personal issues. Even though I love writing, I don't always feel like it. You know what? I do it anyway and so should you. Your goal is to take bite sized pieces of the apple until it is finally consumed. So, dig deep and take action.

Execution helps you build trust in yourself and brings you closer to your desired outcome, as well as reflect successful past performance, bringing you one step closer to your desired outcome. When I was half way through writing this book, my writing was full of surprises. This was something I had to force myself to do for a couple of months but now writing has become the best part. The act of writing becomes its own reward.

Be Afraid of Not Getting your Writing Done

Although we're only born with two fears - the fear of falling and the fear of loud noises - research shows that the number of things we fear increases as we get older. Here are seven of the common fears we all may experience before and while writing our first book.

1. My writing won't be very good.
2. Nobody will want to read my book.
3. I will be judged and receive negative reviews.
4. It won't be a best-seller.
5. Fear of writer's block.
6. Fear of rejection.
7. Fear of failure.

Some of us are even afraid of saying what we are afraid of!

How Steve Jobs Faced His Fears

Whether it's touching a spider, making a speech or asking for a date, societal conditioning makes us fear rejection and failure. Every time he was faced with a big choice, Steve Jobs asked himself, "What would I do if this was the last day of my life?"

He met his wife Laurene like that. Jobs was giving a university address and Laurene was sitting in the audience. He fell for her and wanted to take Laurene out for dinner that very night, but he was afraid she would say no and kidded himself that he had to attend a business meeting. On his way back to his car, Jobs asked himself, "What would I do if this was the last day of my life?" He ran back to the auditorium, found Laurene and took her out to dinner. They remained together until he died. At his funeral, Jobs ensured that everyone in attendance received a copy of the book, Paramahansa Yogananda's The Autobiography of a Yogi. One of the key pillars of this book is the concept of detached engagement. This in essence means:

- *forget about what might happen*
- *focus solely on the task at hand, and*
- *emerge the other side of your fear.*

If fear shows up, you need to focus on what you want and why you are writing.

Brace Yourself for Your Editing

This is one tip I would have loved to be aware of prior to writing this book. We all hope to hear that our book is one of the best books ever to cross the desk of our editor. However, in most cases it's likely that there is a lot of work and changes to be made. For me this felt personal to start with, so I had to change the way I felt and thought about the feedback I was getting. I decided to embrace it in the knowledge that the person giving the feedback wanted to make the book the best it can be. I started to accept that there will always be some truth in the feedback. My attitude is, it's simply my writing, it either works or it doesn't work and I can always change it!

My top tip, based on my experience, is to get all or certainly the majority of your first draft written before you have it edited properly. I have had my book critiqued and edited on nearly a weekly basis and in hindsight it held things up for me and sometimes stopped me feeling as creative as I hoped. It also caused me confusion. The fact is that every manuscript will benefit from a good edit. You have to adopt the mindset that your manuscript is a work in progress and when you submit your first draft, expect the worse.

Be grateful for the feedback in the knowledge that it will add important value to your finished book.

Also consider that no matter how good the editor, or reviewer, they too are not always right. Never change anything that you really want to remain in your book.

You do not have to accept all the recommended edits. Remember this is your book.

We Get What We Focus On

A story about Mel Fisher, 1922-1998, born in Indiana and a dive shop pioneer in California, an American treasure hunter, and best known for finding the 1622 wreck of the Nuestra Señora de Atocha'.

Mel Fisher believed the Spanish ship, the Atocha had sunk somewhere off the coast of Florida. His only clue was a tiny bit of documentation that someone had stumbled across accidentally in a Spanish archive.

For sixteen years, Fisher searched for the ship spending nearly 16 million dollars. He found only a few artefacts near the surface of the ocean floor. Many people spoke out against Fisher's scant discoveries, saying that the artefacts were fake and that Fisher was just trying to recoup his losses. He got further and further into debt, but refused to stop searching. There was tremendous pressure from his investors and the public to give up the search. His crew went sixteen weeks without being paid, continuing only because of Fisher's conviction.

During one expedition, Fisher's son, daughter-in-law and another diver drowned. He refused to give up. His philosophy continued to be, "Today is the day."

Ten years to the day after his son's death, Fisher found the Spanish galleon Nuestra Señora de Atocha. He discovered the wreck on July 20, 1985. The estimated US$450 million cache recovered, known as 'The Atocha Motherlode' included 40 tons of gold and silver; there were some 114,000 of the Spanish silver coins known as 'pieces of eight', gold coins, Colombian emeralds, gold and silver artefacts and 1000 silver ingots. Large as it was, this was only roughly half of the treasure that went down with the Atocha.

The treasure is priceless in terms of historical and cultural value. It was the single largest treasure find ever.

Do you feel you need help with your mindset?

If so, I recommend reading, *Mindset* by Carol Dweck and, *The Chimp Paradox* by Professor Steve Peters.

Chapter Six: Are You Writing or Waiting?

*"Those who write are writers.
Those who wait are waiters."*
A. Lee Martinez, American fantasy and science fiction author.

Your First Draft

Nearly all good writing begins with a poor first draft. You need to get started somewhere. Start by getting anything down on paper, do not worry about spelling, punctuation or grammar; simply write. A great example of this is when I sent my coach Wendy, the first draft of Chapter Four. It was like going back to school when you have handed in the homework that you feel you have nailed, to have it returned to you with a big fat D. This was tough for me because of my perfectionism. I naively thought that my first draft would be all I needed. It took me nearly two weeks to get back to writing and I only did when I acknowledged that it was merely a first draft. All good writers write poor first drafts.

This is how they end up with good second drafts and fantastic third drafts. Rough drafts are meant to be rough.

Writing your first draft is much like watching a child develop from a baby into an adult. You never know exactly how they are going to turn out and you are not supposed to. When writing your first draft, focus on writing for yourself. Even successful authors struggle with which words to use and what to write next. However they will put words down and keep going. A seasoned author will not look back until they have written the entire first draft. A seasoned author knows to keep the drama on the page.

Good editing will always help ensure that your reader will understand you. Writers write for themselves and editors edit to ensure the readers have the best experience from what writers have written. I first discovered this life changing story seventeen years ago on the Internet. It was first named, *What Special Someday Are We Saving For?* by Ann Wells of Laguna Niguel, whose thirty-two year old newspaper essay about loss and cherishing each day has been reborn on the Internet. Wells penned the column a couple of years after her sister unexpectedly died and several years before she lost her husband.

Her work somehow made its way to the Internet, where it moves by e-mail, compliments of the forward button and has been renamed, *A Story to Live By*. Wells, a retired secretary and occasional freelancer was stunned that the essay, first published in The Times in April 1985, has been zipping through cyberspace. She doesn't even have e-mail. "I'm as surprised as anyone," Wells said.

A Story to Live By
By Ann Wells, Los Angeles Times.

My brother-in-law opened the bottom drawer of my sister's bureau and lifted out a tissue wrapped package. "This," he said, "is not a slip. This is lingerie." He discarded the tissue and handed me the slip. It was exquisite, silk, handmade and trimmed with a cobweb of lace. The price tag with an astronomical figure on it was attached. "Jan bought this the first time we went to New York, at least eight or nine years ago. She never wore it. She was saving it for a special occasion. Well, I guess this is the occasion." He took the slip from me and put it on the bed with the other clothes we were taking to the mortician.

His hands lingered on the soft material for a moment and then he slammed the drawer shut and turned to me. "Don't ever save anything for a special occasion. Every day you are alive is a special occasion."

I remembered those words through the funeral and the days that followed when I helped him and my niece attend to all the sad chores that follow an unexpected death. I thought about them on the plane returning to California from the Midwest where my sister's family lived. I thought about all the things that she hadn't seen or heard or done. I thought about the things she had done without realizing they were special.

I'm still thinking about his words and they've changed my life. I'm reading more and dusting less. I'm sitting on the deck and admiring the view without fussing about the weeds in the garden. I'm spending more time with my family and friends and less time in committee meetings. Whenever possible, life should be a pattern of experience to savour, not endure. I'm trying to recognize these moments now and cherish them.

I'm not saving anything; we use our good china and crystal for every special event. I wear my good blazer to the market if I feel like it. My theory is if I look prosperous, I can shell out US$28.49 for one small bag of groceries without wincing. I'm not saving my good perfume for special parties; clerks in hardware stores and tellers in banks have noses that function as well as my party going friends.

'Someday' and 'one of these days' are losing their grip on my vocabulary. If it's worth seeing or hearing or doing, I want to see and hear and do it now. I'm not sure what my sister would have done had she known that she wouldn't be here for the tomorrow we all take for granted. I think she would have called family members and a few close friends. She might have called a few former friends to apologize and mend fences for past squabbles. I like to

think she would have gone out for a Chinese dinner, her favourite food. I'm guessing. I'll never know.

It's those little things left undone that would make me angry if I knew that my hours were limited. Angry because I put off seeing good friends who I was going to get in touch with – someday. Angry because I hadn't written certain letters that I intended to write one of these days. Angry and sorry that I didn't tell my husband and daughter often enough how much I truly love them. I'm trying very hard not to put off, hold back, or save anything that would add laughter and lustre to our lives.

And every morning when I open my eyes, I tell myself that it is special.

Write Now, Procrastinate Later

Agatha Christie only wrote her first book as the result of a challenge from her sister Madge. She received rejection letters for five years between finishing her first book and seeing it published. Five years! She went on to publish ninety one books, amassing more than £1.5 billion in book sales. She was the first crime writer to have 100,000 copies of ten of her titles published by Penguin on the same day in 1948; *A Penguin Million*. She holds The Guinness Book of World Records title of World's Best-selling Author.

Writing your first book is uncomfortable and takes time and money, not to mention the energy. Convincing yourself that it will be worth it will be the hardest part of writing your book. Writing is a personal process that leaves you feeling vulnerable. It is far easier to simply dream about writing rather than to actually write. It's human behaviour to procrastinate. Successful authors develop a laser like focus when it comes to writing their books. The intention of this chapter is to give you the confidence to write.

Are you ready to commit to writing on a regular basis?
I believe you can write a great book, do you? Let's start writing then.

The Four Magic Letters of Writing…Do It

"We are all apprentices in a craft where no one ever becomes a master."
Ernest Hemingway

You need to commit to writing a great book, understanding that the only way to get good is to write. Do it because you love it and want to get your message out. You will find that most best-selling books are an enthusiastic conversation on paper and the author is talking to one person who they really like and care about and they want to share the information with. Always write the way you want to sound, not like anyone else would sound. Be yourself, let it be you speaking. Stacy Nelson, author of, *Writing the Damn Book* says, "Being ready is a lie. We're never ready. If it's not scary, we're not writing. Sit back down and write."

I am frequently asked, "How long will it take to write my book?"

My answer is, "However long you decide it's going to take?"

Getting Into the Flow

When writing never force it, let it flow. Sometimes you will get stuck; for me whenever it's not flowing I get up and have a walk around. I also create a time of silence. To create a time of silence takes a second. A second is a drop of time... a drop of time through which I step to renew myself deep inside. Follow your breath for a while; it will ground you in a beautiful silence.

What gets you into the writing flow?

For example, I treat my writing like my Yoga and for me attending four or five Yoga classes each week means I have to prepare for them, as the list below demonstrates.

- I plan which classes I will attend.
- I book these classes online.
- I put on my Yoga clothes.
- I drive to the Yoga venue.
- I get out my Yoga tools, mat, block and band.
- I have a fantastic Yoga hour.

It is exactly the same with my writing.
- I plan which days I will write.
- I plan when and for how long my session will be.
- I plan what I will write.
- I go to my writing venue for that day.
- I get out my writing tools, favourite pen and moleskin journal.
- I write.

For me my Yoga is non-negotiable. There are days when my body craves it and it is pure bliss. There are other days when my body resists it and most poses are a challenge. There is no right time or right mood. I simply do it. We need the same commitment to our writing.

Location, Location, Location

Find out what works for you. Another aspect that works for me is to be totally on my own so there are no distractions; I am currently writing this chapter on a Bank Holiday Monday evening in my office with some inspirational soft music in the background. Find somewhere that feels comfortable to write the majority of your content; it could be a library, a special room at home, an office, or a hotel room with a stunning view overlooking the sea. The key is to get comfortable.

I Don't Feel Like It

> *"Being in the mood to write is a luxury not a necessity."*
> **Julia Cameron**

Sometimes we simply don't feel like writing; when this happens you usually try to rely on willpower to get yourself back on track. If that isn't working, I have another suggestion. Take another look at the statement, "I Don't Feel Like It"; the answer is right there.

The answer is to get yourself to feel differently; to feel like doing what you have to do.

How? By using your senses to trigger your feelings.

- Create a vision board to inspire you with images of your dreams and goals.
- Create a playlist of music to get you in the right mood to do what you need to do.
- Engage your sense of smell by using oils or scented candles.
- Write using a great pen and nice notebook so you feel more connected to your work.

My point is, when we don't feel like it, we can wait until we do feel like it or we can take steps to have ourselves feel like it.

Other Aspects to Think About

The more time you spend writing, the more successful you will become. How much time do you waste in a week? Use this time to write. Time must be grabbed. Find what gets you into the right frame of mind to write; some authors rest or meditate before going into a session. What works for me is to look through my research and notes for five or ten minutes before I put pen to paper. I am always thinking, "How will this help people?"

Depending on the content of your book and the genre, you should always consider how you get the reader emotionally engaged? Will they cry, smile, laugh or take action? When I write I am 'old' school; I like to put pen to paper first, normally into a nice moleskin journal. The next step is to get it onto a Word document. I also number my pages in the journal because it gives me a structure and helps me to keep track of how many words I have written; I know it's normally around 250 words per page with my journal.

Measuring Time like Pilots

It would be interesting for writers to keep track of time like pilots do. When pilots want to ascertain how long or how seriously someone has been a pilot, they do not ask, "How long have you been flying?" or, "How long have you been a pilot?" They don't care when someone became interested in flying, how many classes and seminars they have attended, how much they know about the physics of flight, or how well they have studied aviation manuals. They don't really care when the person registered for a flight class. Pilots only want to know one thing, "How many hours have you logged flying?" They only need to know how many hours you have sat in a cockpit and flown a plane. The answer says it all. There is a vast difference between an individual who has flown fifteen hours and one who has logged 15,000 hours! As a writer, there is only one thing that counts as hours logged or flight time - actually writing. Research does not count, reading other people's books does not count, nor does planning your book.

Adapted with permission from, *Measuring Time Like Pilots in Dare to Dream and Work to Win* by Dr Tom Barrett.

Warts and All

Your book must be honest and tell of any struggles, as well as the victories. This will make it real and place it in a world where social media is prominent; people don't simply want your book, they also want to know about you. Write with honesty, say what you mean and mean what you say; put it all down. Review your writing regularly and test it in the market place. You need feedback from trusted sources to improve it. Test out some of your content on social media or in the form of a blog to get that feedback.

Practise

Life is all about choices. When you cut away all the junk, every situation is a choice. You choose how you react to situations. You choose how people affect your mood. You choose to be in a good mood or bad mood. You choose whether to write or not. Remember practise helps, and as with exercise, you will probably be sore the first few times, but you will get a little better at it every day that you practise.

Enjoy Your Journey

I remember Jane, a friend of mine sharing a great tip with me about long haul travel. For a long time she dreaded long distance flights considering it to be a waste of her time. But one day she realised that this was actually not only part of her holiday, but also a great time to catch up on her personal writing, her favourite films and television series, or sometimes her sleep. She started to enjoy the journey.

Your writing should be viewed the same. It is a journey to be enjoyed. Know it will not be perfect immediately; try not to take yourself too seriously.

Always Be Ready

Once you start the writing process you will feel inspiration at any time. I remembered the homework feelings while driving to Yoga. I changed a chapter title when I first awoke one morning; I came up with the structure of seven chapters while out walking by the sea. Always be ready to capture these ideas on paper. I have several notebooks at work, in the car, at home and on my telephone. I also record ideas using a Dictaphone. Become a collector of ideas. They may not make it to print in your first book, but maybe make it into your third book!

Every thought can turn into good material; get it all down. I used to think if something was important enough, I'd remember it when I got back home. But after years of making the same mistake and forgetting my inspirations, I now record ideas the minute they come to me because if I don't, I'll forget them. You will too.

Writing Fiction

"Novels are written a sentence at a time."
Julia Cameron

Although this is not my genre, I completed a Writer's Workshop in Las Vegas with the New York Times best-selling science fiction author Steve Alten and I feel it would be remiss of me not to share some of the tips he shared with us.

Steve is best known for his, *Meg Series*, a series of novels set around the fictitious survival of the Megalodon, a giant prehistoric shark. Meg is to be released in 2018 as an American science fiction, action horror film directed by Jon Turteltaub, starring Jason Statham as the lead actor.

The process of writing fiction is the same as writing nonfiction; you have to have done your research, created a plan and an outline. With your story you have to have a beginning, middle and an end. Something has to happen on every page to keep the reader engaged. Finding out what happens will drive people through the book and will bring them back for more books. My daughter Reannon once told me how she began a book and was so engrossed in the story that she read the last chapter before finishing the book to find out how the story ended. You have to be a storyteller who can paint pictures with your words. What is the reader seeing? Smelling? Hearing? Doing?

Most fiction writers write what they like to read and will sometimes build characters into their story from their own life experiences. They write for their ideal reader, the reader who really understands them.

Have You Ever Driven a Car at Night?

"Writing a novel is like driving a car at night. You can see only as far as your headlights, but you can make the whole trip that way."
E. L. Doctorow,
best-selling American history novelist.

You don't have to see the final destination; you only have to see three or four feet ahead of you. This is fantastic advice for writing any book.

Develop Your Characters, Then the Plot

Research your characters. Who is this woman or man and why are they interesting enough to be written about? A whole book is going to be written about them, why? What are their problems? Where are they going? What motivates them?

You have to be able to invent people who didn't exist and don't exist; who maybe do things that have never happened. You have to use your creative imagination. Your characters must have some light and dark in them, they must have flaws, as all of us do.

Who are your main characters and why?

A Formula Can Be a Great Way to Start Your Plot

Steve Alten uses a formula when writing a story, following the ABDCE as below.

- Action.
- Background.
- Development.
- Climax.
- Ending.

He starts with action that is compelling enough to draw us in and to make us want to know more. The background is where you get to know who the people are, and how they came to be in the story. Then he develops the characters, so the reader learns what they care most about. The plot will then grow out of this. He moves them along until everything comes together in the climax of the book, after which things are now different for the main characters. Which brings us to the ending, how do we feel about who these people are now? What are they left with? What happened, and what did it all mean?

Great Resources for Writing Fiction

- *The Artist's Way,* Julia Cameron.
- *The Writer's Journey,* Christopher Vogler.
- *On Writing: A Memoir Of The Craft,* Stephen King.
- *Bird by Bird,* Anne Lamott.

Keep Going Until You Feel Proud

Writing your first book can be both exciting and daunting at the same time, and according to author Jeff Goins, this never goes away. You are always learning how to write a book.

Many first time authors fear they will not be able to finish a book. They are afraid they do not have what it takes to become good enough, and they are also terrified that they do have what it takes and that they could actually become a successful writer. This fear can be chased away quite simply by observing how the best-selling authors do it. They write day after day and at the weekends.

It is similar to the difference between the marathon runner and the person who has merely purchased their new trainers with the goal of completing a marathon, someday. Top marathon runners go through a rigorous step-by-step training process to build up their strength and stamina. Similarly, best-selling authors have trained their minds to produce content at will, whenever and wherever they sit down to write. They can shut out all distractions. They don't wait to be in the perfect writing mood and they do not fear the blank page.

Have a Book Buddy or Book Buddies

It is par for the course with writing that you will have bad days. It can become very lonely on these days. If you have a writing buddy or buddies however, you will always have someone to talk to, someone who will understand your frustration and feelings and someone you can trust. On a bad day you will probably not want a lot of advice. You simply need some empathy and to know there are people who have confidence in you. A buddy or buddies can offer exactly that; as well as an author coach who believes in you and your book.

You Have to Read This Book!

Why do some books outsell others? Here's what I have found has helped to significantly increase book sales.

- It is unique and has current information that is in demand, but that cannot be found anywhere else.
- It has an entertaining and compelling story.
- The author is a well-known celebrity, or a well-known author with a large existing following and a large platform.

- The content is good and the book sells well and people start talking about it and telling other people via word of mouth and social media.

For most first time authors, the goal is to get people talking about you and your book for the right reasons. When someone tells a friend or colleague, "they must read this book" it becomes a very powerful marketing tool. My company Knowledge Is King attends more than 200 events, conferences and trainings a year, ranging from 100 attendees to 20,000. Quite often one of the successful trainers or leaders will promote a good book from the stage as part of their keynote speech. The massive difference this can have on book sales is incredible. Never underestimate the power of word of mouth.

What will be your book's USP - unique selling point - to grab your reader's attention?

A true story that resonated with me about James Corden

In between the success of Gavin and Stacey and Carpool Karaoke, The Late Late Show host, James Corden suffered several career setbacks. These film and television flops sent Corden into a downward spiral and he turned to alcohol and a series of messy relationships.

"Loads of people around me were telling me how great I was and I believed them. But the public weren't buying what I had written," said Corden.

"Suddenly, I realised the work I was doing simply wasn't good enough. I wasn't taking enough care and was cutting corners. As soon as I refocused on producing the best quality work that I could, the success came back," he concluded.

Do the job properly. Go deeper. Make it a word of mouth best-seller. Keep writing until it is a book somebody wants to give to their best friend. When it meets these criteria, then it's time to publish.

Discipline Yourself to Write

Discipline is the difference between being in control of your future and letting your environment dictate your destiny. Discipline means freedom and happiness. It gives you the ability to do what you want to do because you know you can learn how to achieve anything you set your mind to. Discipline teaches you how to control you thoughts - and how to be happy in any situation - to visualise positive emotions and trigger an optimistic mood. Discipline builds self-confidence, mental and physical strength and inspires you to grow as a human being. With growth comes the ability to enjoy life in a deeper, more meaningful way.

Anyone can develop discipline. It is a skill that's not complicated. You simply have to train yourself for it and below is an eleven step process on how to do it.

1. Set big goals – when you challenge yourself to achieve big goals, you really dedicate yourself to the craft of writing. The more time you spend on it, the harder it becomes to quit. Once you have spent so much time and effort on it, if you quit it will all have been for nothing. The bigger the goal the more invested you become.

2. Set clear goals – clearly define what your goal means to you and what you will specifically do to achieve it. If you set a goal to write your book in three months for example, will you write every day? At what time and for how long? If there is no clear goal you will not create the specific steps you need to achieve it. True success requires in-depth reflection and clarity on what you want to accomplish and also why you want to accomplish it. It also helps make sure it's in line with your core values. Without a true understanding of why you are pursuing a goal, obstacles can easily get in your way, which in turn can deflate your motivation. On the other side of that coin, once you understand the purpose of your goal and it's in line with your values, you will remain motivated and inspired to achieve your dreams.

3. Know that every day matters – when you wake in the morning, do you know what is most important for you to achieve that day? Every goal, every priority, you have set for yourself has to be done. It will determine whether your dream lives or dies. Athletes know if they skip even one training session, they are already behind. They know they could lose a competition that is three months away if they don't do what they said they would; if they are not disciplined.

4. Work the plan – if you want to go to the Olympics, each training session matters, there isn't one that's less important than another. It's the same with your writing. When you start the process, you cannot question it, you cannot hesitate and you cannot back down. You have to work hard every time you write to reach your dream.

5. Do it – have the mentality that no matter what, you will accomplish things when you said you would. You have to create pressure for yourself otherwise nothing will get done. There is good stress and bad stress. Make sure you are working under good stress, butterflies in the stomach and adrenaline, which stimulates you to write.

6. Creating a routine – athletes for example, know what hours they will train, when to break for lunch and when to rest. In their training they know they have a warm up, core training and a cool down period. By following the same routine, it becomes second nature. Planning your own writing routine and sticking to it until it becomes automatic will give you the discipline for your own success.

My two hour, 2,000 word writing sessions look as below:

- 25 minutes of writing = 500 words
- 5 minute rest
- 25 minutes of writing = 500 words
- 5 minute rest
- 25 minutes of writing = 500 words
- 5 minute rest
- 25 minutes of writing = 500 words.

In these two hour sessions I will not answer the telephone or go online. During a Bank Holiday I allocated five hours on the Monday to write with the expectation of getting so much done.

But guess what happened? I somehow used up the whole five hours and wrote only 2,000 words. My experience is that you're probably only going to write a few thousand words in any one day.

7. Commit – be prepared to do whatever it takes, prepared to follow through with it until the end, commit to finish the book.

8. Understand the obstacles – your brain and body will do everything it can to resist change and growth. Be aware that it's natural to feel lazy and undisciplined, but also be aware you can change this with your thoughts.

9. Be in control of your feelings – the toughest part of discipline is maintaining the actions needed to achieve your dream. It requires constant hard work and fighting against instant pleasures. For example, I want or think I want another cup of coffee now! Learn to control the feelings that stop you writing, like tiredness, laziness or self-pity.

10. Enjoy working hard – too many people quit too early. Success in writing is all about persistence, and discipline is what will get you to the finished book and the realisation of the dream. The more you learn about writing and what you are capable of, when you start seeing yourself improve, the results will make you hungry for more. Self-development is an amazing drug.

11. Be patient – good books take time. We expect way too much too soon. We all seem to want things to happen too quickly; do your expectations exceed your results? There is no progress without change, but not all change is progress. Your content will evolve as you grow as an author.

Discipline is a source of power. It is the freedom to put all our energy into creating something meaningful and possibly life changing! It is up to us to choose the life with discipline or without, a life with a goal or without.

What do you choose?

The Benefits of Failure

J. K. Rowling's commencement address at Harvard University, 2014:

"I think it's fair to say that by any conventional measure, a mere seven years after my university graduation day, I had failed on an epic scale. An exceptionally short-lived marriage had imploded and I was jobless, a lone parent and as poor as possible to be in modern Britain without being homeless. Failure meant a stripping away of the inessential. I stopped pretending to myself that I was anything other than what I was and began to direct all my energy into finishing the only work that mattered to me.

- *Having the courage to fail is as vital to a good life as any conventional measure of success.*
- *You might never fail on the scale I did, but some failure in life is inevitable.*
- *It is impossible to live without failing at something.*
- *Failure gave me an inner security that I had never attained by passing examinations.*
- *Failure taught me things about myself that I could have learned no other way.*
- *I discovered that I had a strong will and more discipline than I had suspected."*

Do you think J. K. Rowling could have become as successful without the failures?

J. K. Rowling is the author of the best-selling, *Harry Potter* series of seven books, published between 1997 and 2007, which have sold more than 450 million copies worldwide; are distributed in more than 200 territories; are translated into seventy-eight languages; and have been turned into eight blockbuster films.

The Daffodil Principle
By Jaroldeen Asplund Edwards, 1932-2008,
author of twelve published books.

The Daffodil Principle, originally appeared more than nineteen years ago as a story in her book, *Celebration!* Since then, the story has gained international popularity and been retold innumerable times with its simple message, "Start today, one step at a time, to change your world."

Apply the Daffodil Principle to writing your book.

Several times my daughter telephoned to say, "Mother, you must come see the daffodils before they are gone." I wanted to go, but it was a two hour drive from Laguna to Lake Arrowhead.
"I will come next Tuesday," I promised, a little reluctantly on her third call.

Tuesday dawned cold and rainy. Still, I had promised and so I drove there. When I finally walked into Carolyn's house and hugged and greeted my grandchildren, I said, "Forget the daffodils, Carolyn! The road is invisible in the clouds and fog and there is nothing in the world except you and these children that I want to see bad enough to drive another inch!"

My daughter smiled calmly and said, "We drive in this all the time, Mother."

"Well, you won't get me back on the road until it clears and then I'm heading for home!" I assured her.

"I was hoping you'd take me to the garage to pick up my car."

"How far will we have to drive?"

"Only a few blocks," Carolyn said. "I'll drive. I'm used to this."

After several minutes, I had to ask, "Where are we going? This isn't the way to the garage!"

"We're going to my garage the long way," Carolyn smiled, "by way of the daffodils."

"Carolyn," I said sternly, "please turn around."

"It's all right, Mother, I promise. You will never forgive yourself if you miss this experience."

After about twenty minutes, we turned onto a small gravel road and I saw a small church. On the far side of the church, I saw a hand lettered sign that said, "Daffodil Garden."

We got out of the car and each took a child's hand and I followed Carolyn down the path. We turned a corner of the path and I looked up and gasped. Before me lay the most glorious sight. It looked as though someone had taken a great vat of gold and poured it down the mountain peak and slopes. The flowers were planted in majestic, swirling patterns, great ribbons and swaths of deep orange, white, lemon yellow, salmon pink, saffron and butter yellow. Each different coloured variety was planted as a group so they swirled and flowed like its own river each with their unique hue. There were five acres of flowers.

"Who has done this?" I asked Carolyn.

"It's one woman," Carolyn answered. "She lives on the property. That's her home."

Carolyn pointed to a well-kept A-frame house that looked small and modest in the middle of all that glory. We walked up to the house. On the patio, we saw a poster. "Answers to the questions I know you are asking" was the headline.

The first answer was a simple one, "50,000 bulbs," it read. The second answer was, "One at a time, by one woman. Two hands, two feet and very little brain." The third answer was, "Began in 1958."

There it was, The Daffodil Principle. For me, that moment was a life changing experience. I thought of this woman who I had never met, who, more than forty years before, had begun - one bulb at a time - to bring her vision of beauty and joy to an obscure mountain top. Planting one bulb at a time, year after year, she had changed the world. This unknown woman had forever changed the world in which she lived. She had created something of ineffable and indescribable magnificence, beauty and inspiration.

The principle her daffodil garden taught is one of the greatest principles of celebration. That is, learning to move toward our goals and desires one step at a time - often one baby-step at a time - and learning to love the doing, and learning to use the accumulation of time. When we multiply tiny pieces of time with small increments of daily effort, we too will find we can accomplish magnificent things. We can change the world.

"It makes me sad in a way," I admitted to Carolyn. "What might I have accomplished if I had thought of a wonderful goal thirty-five or forty years ago and had worked away at it, 'one bulb at a time' through all those years? Just think what I might have been able to achieve!"

My daughter summed up the message of the day in her usual direct way. "Start tomorrow," she said.

Chapter Seven: Write Something Worth Reading or Do Something Worth Writing

"Everyone must leave something behind when he dies, my grandfather said. A child or a book or a painting or a house or a wall built or a pair of shoes made. Or a garden planted. Something your hand touched some way so your soul has somewhere to go when you die, and when people look at that tree or that flower you planted, you're there."
Ray Bradbury, American short story author and screenwriter, 1920-2012.

Ray Bradbury's quote has kept me on track throughout writing this book. My intention has always been to write something worth reading.

What inspires you to write?

You Have Finished Your Manuscript!

Congratulations, this sets you apart from 99 percent of other people who want to write a book. It is now time to go back over your manuscript and look at it through the eyes of your reader. You have to try and see things from their perspective. When it comes from their perspective it makes it a manuscript worth reading.

Reggie, the Adopted Labrador

I love this fictional story, which for me alludes to fully understanding how others feel, which in my opinion is the key to writing a great first book.

They told me the big black Lab's name was Reggie, as I looked at him lying in his pen. The shelter was clean, no-kill and the people really friendly. I'd only been in the area for six months, but everywhere I went in the small college town, people were welcoming and open. But something was still missing as I settled in to my new life here and I thought a dog couldn't hurt. Give me someone to talk to and I had seen Reggie's advertisement on the local news.

The shelter said they had received numerous calls right after, but they said the people who had come down to see him didn't look like Lab people, whatever that meant. They must've thought I did.

However, at first, I thought the shelter had misjudged me in giving me Reggie and his things, which consisted of a dog pad, bag of toys almost all of which were brand new tennis balls, his dishes and a sealed letter from his previous owner. Reggie and I didn't really hit it off when we got home. We struggled for two weeks, which is how long the shelter told me to give him to adjust to his new home. Maybe it was the fact that I was trying to adjust, too? Maybe we were too much alike?

For some reason, his stuff, except for the tennis balls (he wouldn't go anywhere without two stuffed in his mouth), got tossed in with all of my other unpacked boxes. I guess I didn't really think he'd need all his old stuff, that I'd get him new things once he settled in. But it became pretty clear pretty soon that he wasn't going to.

I tried the normal commands the shelter told me he knew, ones like "sit" and "stay" and "come" and "heel" and he'd follow them; when he felt like it. He never really seemed to listen when I called his name. Sure, he'd look in my direction after the fourth or fifth time I said it, but he'd simply go back to doing whatever. When I'd ask again, you could almost see him sigh and grudgingly obey.

This wasn't going to work. He chewed a couple of shoes and some unpacked boxes. I was a little too stern with him and he resented it, I could tell. The friction got so bad that I couldn't wait for the two weeks to be up and when it was, I was in full on search mode for my mobile amid all of my unpacked stuff. I remembered leaving it on the stack of boxes for the guest room, but I also mumbled, rather cynically, that the "damn dog probably hid it from me."

Finally I found it, but, I also found his pad and other toys from the shelter. I tossed the pad in Reggie's direction and he snuffed it and wagged, some of the most enthusiasm I'd seen since bringing him home. I called, "Hey, Reggie, you like that? Come here and I'll give you a treat." Instead, he sort of glanced in my direction, maybe glared is more accurate and gave a discontented sigh and flopped down, with his back to me.

"Well, that's not going to do it either," I thought and I dialled the shelter phone number. But suddenly, I hung up when I saw the sealed envelope. I had completely forgotten about that, too.

"Okay, Reggie," I said out loud, "let's see if your previous owner has any advice."

To: whoever gets my dog
Well, I can't say that I'm happy you're reading this, a letter I told the shelter could only be opened by Reggie's new owner. If you're reading this, it means I got back from my last car ride with my Lab after dropping him off at the shelter. He knew something was different. I have packed up his pad and toys before and set them by the back door before a trip, but this time, it's like he knew something was wrong. And something is wrong, which is why I have to try to make it right. So, let me tell you about my Lab in the hopes that it will help you bond with him and he with you.

First, he loves tennis balls. The more the merrier. I think he's part squirrel the way he hordes them. He usually has two in his mouth and he tries to get a third in as well, but he hasn't done it yet. Doesn't matter where you throw them, he'll chase after them, so be careful, don't do it by any roads.

Next, commands. Maybe the shelter staff already told you, but I'll go over them again: Reggie knows the obvious ones, "sit", "stay", "come" and "heel." He knows hand signals, "back" to turn around and go back when you put your hand straight up and "over" if you put your hand out right or left. "Shake" for shaking water off and "paw" for a high-five. He does "down" when he feels like lying down and "ball", "food", "bone" and "treat". I trained Reggie with small food treats. Nothing opens his ears like little pieces of hot dog.

Feeding schedule: twice a day, once about seven in the morning and again at six in the evening. Regular store bought stuff, the shelter has the brand.

He's up on his shots. Call the clinic on 9th Street and update his info with yours. They'll make sure to send you reminders for when he's due. Be forewarned, Reggie hates the vet. Good luck getting him in the car. I don't know how he knows when it's time to go to the vet but he knows.

Finally, give him some time. I've never been married, so it's only been Reggie and me for his whole life. He's gone everywhere with me, so please include him on your daily car rides if you can. He sits well in the backseat and he doesn't bark or complain. He loves to be around people and me most especially, which means this transition is going to be hard, with him going to live with someone new.

That's why I need to share one more bit of info with you.

His name is not Reggie. I don't know what made me do it, but when I dropped him off at the shelter, I told them his name was Reggie. He's a smart dog, he'll get used to it and will respond to it, of that I have no doubt. But I couldn't bear to give them his real name. For me to do that, it seemed so final, that handing him over to the shelter was as good as me admitting that I'd never see him again. And if I end up coming back, getting him and tearing up this letter, it means everything's fine. But if someone else is reading it, well, it means that his new owner should know his real name. It'll help you bond with him.

Who knows, maybe you'll even notice a change in his demeanour if he's been giving you problems. His real name is Tank because that is what I drive. Again, if you're reading this and you're from the area, maybe my name has been on the news. I told the shelter they couldn't make Reggie available for adoption until they received word from my company commander.

See, my parents are gone, I have no siblings, no one I could've left Tank with and it was my only real request of the Army on my deployment to Iraq that they make one telephone call to the shelter, in the event, to tell them that Tank could be put up for adoption. Luckily, my Colonel is a dog guy too, and he knew where my platoon was headed. He said he'd do it personally and if you're reading this, then he made good on his word.

Well, this letter is getting downright depressing, even though, frankly, I'm writing it for my dog. I couldn't imagine if I was writing it for a wife and kids and family. But Tank has been my family for the last six years, almost as long as the Army has been my family. I hope and pray you make him part of your family and he will adjust and come to love you the same way he loved me. That unconditional love from a dog is what I take with me to Iraq as an inspiration to do something selfless, to protect innocent people from those who would do terrible things and to keep those terrible people from coming over here. If I have to give up Tank to do it, I am glad to have done so. He is my example of service and of love. I hope I honoured him by my service to my country and comrades.

All right, that's enough. I deploy this evening and have to drop this letter off at the shelter. I don't think I'll say another goodbye to Tank, though. I cried too much the first time. Maybe I'll peek in on him and see if he finally got that third tennis ball in his mouth.

Good luck with Tank. Give him a good home and give him an extra kiss goodnight - every night - from me.

Thank you.   Paul Mallory

I folded the letter and slipped it back in the envelope. Sure, I had heard of Paul Mallory, everyone in town knew him, even new people like me. Local kid, killed in Iraq a few months ago and posthumously earning the Silver Star when he gave his life to save three buddies. Flags had been at half-mast all summer.

I leaned forward in my chair and rested my elbows on my knees, staring at the dog.
"Hey, Tank," I said quietly.
The dog's head whipped up, his ears cocked and his eyes bright.
"C'mere boy."

He was instantly on his feet, his nails clicking on the hardwood floor. He sat in front of me, his head tilted searching for the name he hadn't heard in months.
"Tank," I whispered. His tail swished. I kept whispering his name and each time, his ears lowered, his eyes softened and his posture relaxed as a wave of contentment seemed to flood him. I stroked his ears, rubbed his shoulders, buried my face into his scruff and hugged him.
"It's me now, Tank, just you and me. Your old pal gave you to me." Tank reached up and licked my cheek. "So, what daya say we play some ball?

His ears perked again. "Yeah? Ball? You like that? Ball?" Tank tore from my hands and disappeared in the next room and when he came back, he had three tennis balls in his mouth.

Makes you think doesn't it?

Your Next Steps

A great tip when your manuscript is finished is to have someone read your book out loud to you, while you make notes. Once your manuscript is finished, you will have completed a first draft, had it edited, revised and completed a second edit and finally finished your third fully edited draft, which is your completed manuscript. I strongly encourage you to employ professional help with the next steps, especially if you wish to be the author of a book that really matters.

Your next steps will be:

- editing
- proofreading
- internal design and typeset
- cover design
- create E-book edition, and
- publish.

You will now have your finished book and your next steps will be:

- selling
- distribution, and
- marketing online and offline.

Editing

A good professional editor is important. The number one way that books are sold is by word of mouth and to write a great book you need a great editor. A good professional editor will cost anything between £500 and £900, depending on the amount of words.

A good professional editor will help you to:

- find your writing style and voice
- structure your chapters and ultimately your book
- stay on task; they hold you accountable
- be creative and to get your message across
- use language properly and to get the right words on the page
- brainstorm when you get lost or stuck, and
- help with both the internal design, cover and back cover text.

Internal Design and Typeset

This is another aspect to research; when you are in a bookstore study the stand out layouts and what makes them stand out? In my research I got familiar with different internal designs, styles and typeset. This helped me to choose the design you are reading. Setting out the interior of your book is one of the most important details of the whole publishing process. Get advice from everyone on your book team, on main headings, headings, subheadings, the different styles of typeface and point size and how to break up your text with paragraphs. Experiment with different fonts and point sizes. My goal for my layout was to increase my reader's enjoyment.

Proofreading

In my opinion you must get your book professionally proofread. A good publisher will only allow a book with near perfect spelling, grammar and punctuation to be published. Think back to when you read a book that had too many mistakes in it? I know how it makes me feel. I also know when I write I am too close to my books to spot the little things. It is okay to have friends and family provide a basic proofread for free to help you before you go to a professional. A little tip here is to get your volunteers to read your book backwards. This will help to highlight more errors.

A good proofreader will not set you back much, probably between £250/£600 and it will generally depend on the length of your book, the complexity of the text and the 'turn around' time. But it's a solid investment and will add value to your book. They will comb through your book several times picking up any typos, grammatical mistakes, inconsistencies and ambiguities, and will usually make the corrections too. They will also help with the flow of your book because they care about their work.

A word of caution - it may be wise to involve the proofreader for one more check after it's been to the typesetter.

Cover and Back Cover Design of Your Book

As we mentioned previously, you must employ a good cover designer, someone who knows your genre and understands the underlying message or story behind your book. Remember, we actually do judge a book by its cover!

Create an E-book Edition

Nowadays there are many electronic formats. It has become common to distribute books, magazines and newspapers to consumers through tablet reading devices. This is a market growing by millions each year and generated by online vendors, such as Apple's iTunes bookstore, Amazon's bookstore for Kindle and books in the Google Play Bookstore. I publish initially on Kindle, Nook, iPad and smartphone. Most publishers of physical books will offer you the opportunity to publish an e-book edition. It is worth doing this with a professional who will duplicate the quality and message of your paper edition.

Publish

You have several choices; to self-publish or to go down the traditional publishing route with a mainstream publisher. In my opinion there has never been a better time to self-publish. I advise authors to self-publish first and when you have built a solid platform and your book is becoming successful, then go to the big publishers.

Here are some points to consider when deciding.

Self-Publishing

With self-publishing you have total control of:

- who publishes your book and when you are published
- your title
- your cover design
- the editing, and
- the profits…it's all yours!

You will be responsible in most parts for selling and marketing your book both online and offline.

Tips for Finding a Good Self-Publishing Company

- Find a self-publisher who specialises in your genre.
- Find out exactly what services you are getting for your money.
- Research their background and check out their published books and the ratings on Amazon.
- Speak to authors who have used their services and obtain their first-hand feedback.

Traditional Publishing

With traditional publishing it can take anything between twelve to eighteen months to have your book published. As a first time author with a traditional publisher you will be doing 70/80 percent of the selling of your book. A traditional publisher will publish and distribute your book. You will be responsible for the majority of sales. You will get around a 10 percent royalty on books sold.

Some of the benefits of going with a traditional publisher are:

- you may get an advance payment
- you will be working with top editors, proofreaders, sales teams and marketers; all with a vested interest in creating your best book

- you harness the credibility and authority of being published by a traditional publisher
- you will gain opportunities to work with the press and media, opportunities to promote yourself and your book, and
- you will have access to your publisher's platform.

The Cab Ride I'll Never Forget
By Kent Nerburn

This is a true story that happened to Kent in Minneapolis, Minnesota, USA in the early 1980s. At the time, he was working as a driver for the Yellow Cab Company and worked what he called, 'the dog shift' overnight. The story was originally published in a book by Kent Nerburn, *Make Me an Instrument of Your Peace*, published by Harper, San Francisco.

There was a time in my life, twenty years ago, when I was driving a cab for a living. It was a cowboy's life, a gambler's life, a life for someone who wanted no boss, constant movement and the thrill of a dice roll every time a new passenger got into the cab. What I didn't count on when I took the job was that it was also a ministry; because I drove the night shift, my cab became a rolling confessional. Passengers climbed in, sat behind me in total anonymity and told me about their lives.

We were like strangers on a train, the passengers and I, hurtling through the night, revealing intimacies we would never have dreamed of sharing during the brighter light of day. I encountered people whose lives amazed me, ennobled me, made me laugh and made me weep.

And none of those lives touched me more than that of a woman I picked up late on a warm August night. I was responding to a call from a small brick fourplex in a quiet part of town. I assumed I was being sent to pick up some partiers, or someone who had had a fight with a lover, or someone going off to an early shift at some factory in the industrial part of town.

When I arrived at the address, the building was dark except for a single light in a ground floor window. Under these circumstances, many drivers honk once or twice, wait a short minute, then drive away. Too many bad possibilities awaited a driver who went up to a darkened building at 2:30am in the morning. But I had seen too many people trapped in a life of poverty who depended on the cab as their only means of transportation. Unless a situation had a real whiff of danger, I always went to the door to find the passenger. It might, I reasoned, be someone who needed my assistance. Would I not want a driver to do the same if my mother or father had called for a cab?

So, I walked to the door and knocked.
"Just a minute," answered a frail and elderly voice. I heard the sound of something being dragged across the floor. After a long pause, the door opened. A small woman somewhere in her eighties stood before me. She was wearing a print dress and a pillbox hat with a veil pinned on it, like you might see in a costume shop or a Goodwill store or in a 1940s movie. By her side was a small nylon suitcase. The sound had been her dragging it across the floor.

The apartment looked as if no one had lived in it for years. All the furniture was covered with sheets. There were no clocks on the walls, any knick-knacks or utensils on the counters. In the corner was a cardboard box filled with photos and glassware.

"Would you carry my bag out to the car?" she said. "I'd like a few moments alone. Then, if you could come back and help me? I'm not very strong."

I took the suitcase to the cab and then, returned to assist the woman. She took my arm and we walked slowly toward the curb. She kept thanking me for my kindness.

"It's nothing," I told her. "I try to treat my passengers the way I would want my mother to be treated."

"Oh, you're such a good boy," she said. Her praise and appreciation were almost embarrassing.

When we got in the cab, she gave me an address and then asked, "Could you drive through downtown?"

"It's not the shortest way," I answered.

"Oh, I don't mind," she said. "I'm in no hurry. I'm on my way to a hospice."

I looked in the rear-view mirror. Her eyes were glistening.

"I don't have any family left," she continued. "The doctor says I should go there. He says I don't have very long."

I quietly reached across and shut off the meter. "What route would you like me to go?" I asked.

For the next two hours we drove through the city. She showed me the building where she had once worked as an elevator operator. We drove through the neighbourhood where she and her husband had lived when they were first married. She had me pull up in front of a furniture warehouse that had once been a ballroom where she went dancing as a girl. She also had me slow in front of a particular building or corner and sat staring into the darkness, saying nothing.

As the first hint of sun was creasing the horizon, she suddenly said, "I'm tired. Let's go now."

We drove in silence to the address she had given me. It was a low building, like a small convalescent home, with a driveway that passed under a portico. Two orderlies came out to the cab as soon as we pulled up. Without waiting for me, they opened the door and began assisting the woman. They were solicitous and intent, watching her every move. They must have been expecting her; perhaps she had telephoned them right before we left.

I opened the trunk and took the small suitcase up to the door. The woman was already seated in a wheelchair.

"How much do I owe you?" she asked, reaching into her purse.

"Nothing," I said.

"You have to make a living," she answered.

"There are other passengers," I responded.

Almost without thinking, I bent and gave her a hug. She held on to me tightly.

"You gave an old woman a little moment of joy," she said. "Thank you."

There was nothing more to say. I squeezed her hand

once and walked out into the dim morning light.

Behind me, I heard the door shut. It was the sound of the closing of a life.
I did not pick up any more passengers that shift. I drove aimlessly, lost in thought. For the remainder of that day, I could hardly talk.

What if that woman had gotten an angry driver, or one who was impatient to end his shift? What if I had refused to take the run, or had honked once and driven away? What if I had been in a foul mood and had refused to engage the woman in conversation?
How many other moments like that had I missed or failed to grasp?
We are so conditioned to think that our lives revolve around great moments. But great moments often catch us unawares.

When that woman hugged me and said I had brought her a moment of joy, it was possible to believe that I had been placed on earth for the sole purpose of providing her with that last ride. I do not think that I have ever done anything in my life that was any more important.

What if your first book turned out to be one of the most important things you do in your life?

Persistence

Some of us will hit a wall with our writing. It is easy to consider that to be the end of the road and to give up. Only the most stubborn people among us will persevere long enough to finish the book. Think of the Wright brothers, trying to get people in the air. Can you imagine what their peers said? Today we can't imagine a world without airplanes. There is a Chinese bamboo tree that thrives in Indonesia. Planting, watering and fertilising the seed for five years yields no results, but shortly after that the tree sprouts and grows at least ninety feet in six weeks!

Writing a great first book is much like the growing process of the Chinese bamboo tree.

It can be discouraging.

We seemingly do things right, but sometimes nothing happens. For those people who do the right things and are not discouraged and persist, good things will happen; keep showing up and writing.

It is never too late to write your first book. Louise Hay started Hay House publishing at the age of sixty and wrote her last book at age ninety. Her best-selling book, *You Can Heal Your Life*, sold more than forty million copies.

Gratitude

I am very grateful to so many people in my life.

My parents, Wilf and Rita; thank you for your constant support and for instilling my love of reading and my entrepreneurial mindset at an early age.

My children, Asa, Reannon and Lyle; you have always been the wind beneath my wings.

My granddaughters, Lyla and Mya; you remind me constantly of how important family is to living a good life.

I have many great customers who are also friends; your support and comments are why I write and read books.

My beta readers, Bernie and Fran; thank you for your honesty and holding me accountable.

My author coach and professional editor, Wendy; thanks for keeping me on track.

My proofreader, Meg; whose attention to detail is phenomenal and with whom I share a passion for Cornwall.

All the inspiring authors who have helped to shape my life during the past two decades.

And of course, Carola; thank you for introducing me to real love.

To You, the Reader

I am thrilled with the thought that this book may offer inspiration, insight and enrichment to you. This was my goal. What is interesting to me is that I merely started writing and let it unfold. Books have their own plan. Let them evolve.

Has it inspired you to take the idea of yours and turn it into your book?

It is now time for you to take action. If you follow the practical advice in this book and take the achievable actions suggested, you will write a great first book. I know they work because I have used them all to create this book. We all experience moments of inspiration; where a brilliant light shines through the ordinary moments in our normal days. They come unsolicited and unannounced and provide us with the gift of significance and, if we are lucky, the opportunity to serve. Writing and reading feeds the soul. It is important to remember that these are gifts and we cannot receive them unless we are open to receive them. We need to listen closely, watch closely, and take care not to rush past or through them when they arrive.

Always remember that your book can change someone else's life.

What gift will your book share with your readers?

One of the most enjoyable parts of writing a book is connecting with the readers. Please feel free to get in touch with me if you'd like to. I would love to hear all about your book and to see if I can further support you. If you are interested in my coaching programme for authors, where we go from idea to published book in four months, please ask and I will send you details.

Email: barry@knowledgeisking.co.uk

Phone: + 44 (0)1491 201530

Further Reading

Please consider these titles for further insight and inspiration.

The Artist's Way, Julia Cameron… required reading for everyone.

The Writer's Journey, Christopher Vogler… fiction writers.

On Writing: A Memoir of the Craft, Stephen King… fiction writers.

Bird by Bird, Anne Lamott… required reading for everyone.

The Right to Write, Julia Cameron… required reading for everyone.

Your Story, Joanne Fedler… non-fiction.

You Must Write A Book, Honoree Corder… non-fiction.

Writing The Damn Book, Stacy Nelson… non-fiction.

Thank you for buying this book.